Marshall Keeble

ROLL JORDAN ROLL

A Biography of Marshall Keeble

by

J. E. CHOATE

GOSPEL ADVOCATE COMPANY
Nashville, Tennessee
1974

DEDICATION

A. M. Burton, N. B. Hardeman, and B. C. Goodpasture

IN MEMORIAM

To three Negro preachers long since forgotten save for a circle of their family and friends, the fact is generously acknowledged by Marshall Keeble that the first part of the story of his life is told in the persons of S. W. Womack, Alexander Cleveland Campbell, and G. P. Bowser.

CONTENTS

INTRODUCTION

"We spend our years as a tale that is told"; friends of the Negro evangelist wrote this statement on his seventy-sixth anniversary. And what a beautiful tale has been told in the life of Brother Marshall Keeble. It is the purpose of this book to tell that story.

Without doubt Keeble is the best known member of the church of Christ. His reputation, unlike many leaders of the church, transcends racial boundaries. It would be difficult to find an adult member of the church of Christ who has not heard of him. He has converted more people than any preacher—lettered or unlettered, in the churches of Christ irrespective of race. He never attended college as he says "to get his brain expanded," but no "educated preacher" can even come close to him in preaching the gospel. People come in vast numbers to hear him—not because he is a Negro, but because they are anxious to hear what he has to say.

Several years ago, he was on his way to lecture in George Pepperdine College. A friend wished him to speak to a high school student body in Tucson, Arizona. The principal was not much in favor of the idea until he learned he was President of The Nashville Christian Institute. Keeble said: "I didn't look like much; but when I got up, he didn't want me to stop. I just charmed him—he was a surprised man." The students gave him a great ovation.

No other Negro preacher enjoys a national reputation of equal respect with that of Marshall Keeble; nor has any other preacher been so universally accepted by the members of his religious fellowship. Numerous attempts are made to explain him, and his anecdotes are endlessly repeated. Few criticisms are turned in his direction. The one heard most often sees too much of the "clown" in him; however, this fails to stand upon close examination.

The Restoration Movement is largely associated with a few men who started the plea to restore the patterns of New Testament Christianity. The names of Alexander Campbell, Barton W. Stone, Tolbert Fanning, and David Lipscomb are generally associated with this movement in church history. Marshall Keeble is a vital personality in that evangelistic movement which began in the early part of the nineteenth century.

Furthermore, Keeble is the only Negro preacher to participate in the Restoration Movement on a national basis. There are other outstanding preachers among the Negroes, but none have reached the stature of Keeble. G. P. Bowser was the only other Negro preacher to enjoy a wide popularity within the Restoration Movement.

Keeble was featured, March 29, 1964, in the "Magazine" section of *The Nashville Tennessean.* The feature writer observed—"from whichever side of the theological fence he is viewed, Evangelist Keeble is incredible." How true this is even to those who have known him the longest and who are ever amazed. Though they understand his sermons, they cannot analyze the man. Often quoted, it is impossible to imitate him. Not even Keeble tries to explain his power as a preacher, but what he does is no mystery. Like Jesus he says —"Without a parable I never speak." A part of the secret of his success is in the simplifying of his lessons so as to make them clear to the illiterate persons in his audience. Like the clear waters coursing down the slopes of Mount Hermon, words roll from his soul to stir the hearts of all who come to hear him.

He has preached and travelled everywhere. Dance halls, tobacco warehouses, little log cabins in the South, lumber sheds, brush arbors, the backward "bush county" of Africa, and palatial air-conditioned municipal auditoriums have been among the settings for his sermons. Keeble said that he has preached in the South with as many as twenty babies lying on pallets around the pulpit. He stepped all around them; but he said, "I never stepped on one of them when someone came to obey the gospel."

Snow was raked off the tent in Birmingham, Alabama, for him to preach and a potbellied stove was set up in a tent in Nashville, Tennessee, during chilly October evenings. His brethren have chopped through ice so Keeble could baptize. He has baptized in the great rivers of this nation and in two oceans and stood on the banks of the Jordan River and walked the road Paul traveled to Damascus.

This Negro preacher has traveled by land, sea, and air. He told once about crossing the flooded Cumberland River in a canoe on his way to a preaching appointment: "We were out in the swift current. I never saw such paddling. I was so scared, I couldn't even talk."

One of his brethren said: "Brother Keeble, I've crossed the

Lillie May Burton and A. M. Burton

river when it was higher than this." But that comforted Keeble little till that skiff touched land.

He was no more at ease when he flew in a "prop" plane from Los Angeles to keep a Lipscomb Lectureship appointment. When Hugh H. Tiner told him how fast that plane would go to Nashville, Keeble remarked: "That fast train that brought me out here was too fast for me." Keeble has gone mule back, by wagon, and in Chevrolets and Cadillacs. The Bible didn't tell him how to go, or he would had gladly obeyed that injunction. His beloved Bible told him to go into all the world, and he has now done that. The Negro evangelist has preached from the Golden Gate Bridge to New York Harbor, and in faraway Korea.

Keeble spoke annually in the Tennessee State Prison for about thirty years to some 2000 prisoners. One time five white men and five Negroes came forward to be baptized. He converted a man on "death row." His cell was right next to the electric chair. He had to see it everyday. When Keeble offered him the Lord's supper in the shadow of the chair and in the presence of other condemned men, he said it was a good lesson for them. "To see that man doomed to die and so sincere and I know a few more days he's to sit in that chair"; Keeble said, "sometimes he and I both would be crying."

No man in recorded history probably has spoken so many words for Christ as this "ebony" man. Whatever the influence of Keeble may have been in other social circumstances in the post Civil War years is another question without import. The fact is he accepted the challenge to preach to the Negro and received the support of white people to the eminent satisfaction of all.

Some of the Negro acquaintances of Keeble said he "belongs to white people." He added: "I got those white people to help build up those churches. My work has appealed to them. I have nobody to fight. Nothing I am doing they haven't helped me in." He has chilled more than one critical Negro brother: "The white man is your friend and you don't even know it."

Only in recent years have leading preachers among the churches of Christ been made the subjects of master's theses and doctoral dissertations in colleges and universities. Keeble is the first member of his race to become the subject of such studies.

The evangelist has been featured as the main speaker on lectureships in the colleges operated by the members of the churches of Christ for years. One of Keeble's granddaughters was the first Negro student to live on the George Pepperdine College Campus, and among the first to enroll in the college. A citation was presented him in March 24, 1956, by President Hugh H. Tiner during the Pepperdine Fellowship Month which reads in part: "In expression of its appreciation for his bringing multiplied thousands to Christ." This was the first of similar outstanding honors coming from his brethren.

Equal honors have come to Keeble from the citizens of his community. The Business and Professional Women's Club sponsored a weekly program on WLAC featuring some especially prominent Nashvillian. Keeble was honored December 4, 1954, as "The man of the hour."

Governor Frank G. Clement paid him a signal honor, December 6, 1965, when he was appointed "Colonel Aide-De-Camp" on the governor's staff of honorary colonels. He was the first member of his race in Tennessee to be so honored. The appointment was accompanied by a "Certificate of Appreciation" for "His major contributions to civic causes, for benefits to social enrichment, for dedication to Christian leadership, for devotion to international education, and for a life of sacrifice for the Nashville Christian Institute.

Mayor Beverly Briley of Metropolitan Nashville presented on Keeble's birthday, December 7, 1965, a bronze plaque with the inscription: "In grateful recognition of Marshall Keeble for his long time service to his God and to his fellowman, preaching and teaching the gospel, baptizing 30,000 souls and establishing 350 congregations. His life's work including his appointment as President Emeritus of Nashville Christian Institute is a shining example of good citizenship."

Of the many honors appreciated by Keeble over his long life, he enjoys the one conferred on him in 1960 just before he and Lucien Palmer left Africa for the States. The students in the Nigerian Bible College gave them a farewell party which was attended by the local government dignitaries. During the festival Keeble was presented with a robe and made an honorary chief over one of the largest Nigerian tribes. He was presented the "walking cane" of authority by the Paramount Chief.

Whatever honor his brethren could confer on Keeble, they have. On a fund raising tour in 1962, in the company of James O.

Baird, President of Oklahoma Central College, Baird wrote: "Brother Keeble is as remarkable and astounding as ever. Four thousand people came to hear him in Oklahoma City marking the largest gathering of Christian people under one roof at one meeting in the history of our state. Scores of white brethren owe their conversion to him. Almost every Negro congregation in our state was either founded by Brother Keeble or reflects the imprint of his work through someone else. In this sense he is as much like Paul as any man among us today."

Shortly after Clifton L. Ganus, Jr. became president of Harding College in 1965, George S. Benson and Marshall Keeble were accompanied by Willie T. Cato and Carl Robinson on a fund raising tour for the Nashville Christian Institute. President Ganus flew to Dallas, Texas, specifically to confer the honorary doctor's degree on Marshall Keeble. The Certificate reads:

Harding College
Be It Known
To all persons that the President and Trustees of Harding College
in recognition of distinguished attainment have conferred upon
Marshall Keeble
the honorary degree of
Doctor of Laws
with all the Honors, Rights, and Privileges of that degree appertaining. Given at Searcy in the State of Arkansas on this twelfth day of December in the year of our Lord nineteen hundred and sixty-five.

Whenever a Christian college wanted to make sure of a large audience, the key speaking occasion was turned over to Marshall Keeble. When such vast crowds were pressing into the Municipal Auditorium in Lubbock, Texas, the fire marshall finally turned the over flow away. But this is "old shoe" in the Keeble story. The churches of Christ planned a worship service for July 4, 1965, in the World's Fair Singer Bowl, in New York City, Jimmy Allen was the featured speaker. Keeble was present to offer the closing prayer.

A poet wrote a poem about the American pioneers with a line that ran something like this: "Give me men to match my mountains." Words are inadequate to describe Keeble or his life's work. Numerous legends have grown up around Keeble with the hope the legend will match the greatness of the man. The legends may be explained in the sense that they were created to focus the gargantuan achievements of this plain little man, who, in the thirties, wrote the *Advocate* that he had baptized fifteen thousand persons. That number in recent years ranges from thirty to fifty thousand. The number of new congregations attributed to him number three hundred fifty. But no one knows exactly since no records have been kept. But the facts about Keeble are more amazing than the stories told about him.

The "Keeble Story" must begin some place. It actually starts in 1900 when Keeble, then twenty-two years old, was standing on the threshold of a fabulous life. A Negro preacher by the name of Alexander Cleveland Campbell in some fashion came under the influence of David Lipscomb. Campbell had been taught out of the Christian Church by persons unknown. Campbell was later joined by two other North Nashville Negro preachers. One was S. W. Womack, the father-in-law of Marshall Keeble, and G. P. Bowser, who had been an ordained Methodist preacher.

Under the direct influence and tutelage of David Lipscomb and his associates, the three Negro evangelists started the "restoration of New Testament Christanity" in North Nashville. Keeble, a member of the Lea Avenue Christian Church, was a charter member. The life of Marshall Keeble can't be told apart from the work of Campbell, Womack and Bowser, and the white brethren who encouraged them.

CHAPTER I

The Chariots of Israel

No man ever accomplishes anything entirely alone, and the life of Marshall Keeble cannot be separated from the world he grew up in or the people who greatly influenced the course of his life. Marshall Keeble is a living legend. The fictitious and the factual are indistinguishably mingled wherever the Keeble story is told. Fortunately the undistorted facts are known. The life of Keeble may only be comprehended when the antecedents of his life are examined. The reader must patiently study the contents of this chapter to understand the subject of this book.

When the history of the churches of Christ is finally recorded in this century, a handful of white Christians will be remembered for their religious interest in the Negro. And whatever has happened in the story of Restoration History among the churches of Christ is traceable in a full measure to David Lipscomb. Had it not been for David Lipscomb, it is highly unlikely that the preaching of the gospel would have begun as early and prospered so generously. It would be impossible to calculate the influence of David Lipscomb on the whole course of the Restoration of New Testament Christianity. Perhaps the least publicized of Lipscomb's efforts are those among the Negro race. He championed their cause without reservation from his earliest preaching days.

Marshall Keeble identifies three persons responsible for his preaching the gospel to his people—Alexander Cleveland Campbell, S. W. Womack, and G. P. Bowser. They were three Negro preachers living in North Nashville in the neighborhood of the world famed Fisk University. Alexander Cleveland Campbell deserves first honors for starting the Restoration of New Testament Christianity in North Nashville among the Negro race around the turn of this century.

Alexander Cleveland Campbell, his wife, and mother were baptized in Wartrace, Tennessee, by D. M. Keeble, the uncle of Marshall Keeble. Campbell secured work and moved his family to Nashville. They began worshipping in the Lea Avenue Christian Church. Aleck Campbell wore the illustrous name of the great Bethany, West Virginia preacher, educator, and debater of the

1

early nineteeth century, Alexander Campbell, who came to America from Scotland. Alexander Cleveland Campbell went by the name of "Aleck" to all who knew him. To avoid mistaking him for Alexander Campbell of Bethany, West Virginia, he will be identified with his nickname, "Aleck" in all further references to him in this book. Around 1900 Aleck Campbell served as the personal valet of General William Hicks Jackson. General Jackson, after whose family Jackson, Tennessee, was named, was the son-in-law of William Giles Harding, owner of the Belle Meade plantation. Belle Meade was widely known as the "Queen of Tennessee Plantations" before the Civil War and celebrated for its gracious living and social splendor throughout the South.

Aleck Campbell accompanied General Jackson on his numerous trips away from Nashville. He waited on the "General" at home in the Belle Meade Mansion. After Campbell left the services of General Jackson he never held another full time job. All of his time and efforts were spent in preaching the gospel.

It is often said that behind every great man stands a good woman. And it is often the case that some man plays a special role in helping develop another man of superior talents. Keeble named such a man who shaped his life—his father-in-law, S. W. Womack, who made the first and most lasting indelible impressions. The story of the preacher—Marshall Keeble—actually begins when his father bought a home next door to the Womacks.

Unfortunately, little information survives about the family background of S. W. Womack. Womack was married to "Aunt Sally" as she was affectionately known to the family. Two daughters, Philistia and Minnie, lived to be grown; another child, Elnora, died in her infancy. Marshall Keeble married Minnie when he was eighteen. She had finished the Fisk University High School Department. Womack moved to Nashville from a small place called Fosterville in Rutherford County, Tennessee, near Lynchburg.

Womack taught school for a while around Lynchburg. After coming to Nashville he preached full time. Womack followed Aleck Campbell out of the Christian Church, and joined hands with him in launching the Restoration of New Testament Christianity among the Negro people. In this respect they may be compared to Alexander Campbell and Barton W. Stone who spearheaded the initial movement to restore the patterns of New Testament Christianity in the early years of the nineteenth century.

2

G. P. Bowser joined Campbell and Womack a short while after they pulled out of the Christian Church. The influence of Bowser among the Negro disciples in the intervening years has equalled that of Keeble's in some respects. He was the son of Thomas and Elizabeth Charity Bowser. They lived in Hickman and Maury County, Tennessee, the first three years of their married life. They were the parents of two daughters and three sons. When Bowser was three years old, the family moved to Nashville. The mother desired her children to receive a good education. Though Bowser's mother was a member of the Christian church, he joined the A. M. E. Bethel Church at fifteen, and was ordained a minister of the Methodist church at the age of twenty-one. He was educated in Nashville, Tennessee, in Walden University. Bowser met Sam Davis, an ex-slave and a preacher in the Christian Church, who taught Bowser the gospel and convinced him to give up his "denominational" Christianity. Bowser resisted what he called "being baptized again" since he had been baptized into the Methodist church. Later he agreed for Sam Davis to baptize him in the manner set forth in the New Testament.

For more than forty years G. P. Bowser exerted a great force for good among the Negro Christians. His relation to Christian education and religious journalism among Negroes is much like that of David Lipscomb. Lipscomb created the classic concepts of Christian education which are generally accepted among the members of the churches of Christ.

Campbell, Womack, and Bowser were the first Negro preachers to be generally recognized by the white people after the Civil War. They received from them their major support. And it is fortunate for the church historian that the *Gospel Advocate* welcomed their field reports and articles.

The interest of the leading white members of the churches of Christ in the American Negro is not a recent thing. The Restoration Movement was a singular religious phenomenon on the American frontier. The Cumberland Mountain plateau and adjacent regions became strongholds for the Christian Church—or as it was sometimes designated—"the Campbellite Church." Christian Negroes worshipped in the old Cane Ridge meetinghouse in Kentucky where Barton W. Stone preached. Several plantations were located nearby. The plantation owners built a balcony in the Cane Ridge meetinghouse especially for the Negroes. In 1815 a great revival was conducted by the white people at Cane Ridge, and a

3

large number of Negroes were baptized. A congregation of Negro disciples, which is another case in point, was organized in 1816 in Celina, Tennessee. Negro slaves were baptized in the church of Christ in Thyatira, Mississippi, before the Civil War. After the war they established a congregation among themselves.

Worshipping with white people was not without influence on the Negro. The Baptist and Methodist followed the practice of building separate meetinghouses for their servants. The white disciples did not follow suit since their churches were relatively small in membership, and the Negro disciples were encouraged to worship with them. At the close of the Civil War in the summer of 1865, the white disciples of Lynchburg, Tennessee, gave the Negroes their first protracted meeting. The preaching was done by Brethren T. W. Brents, R. B. Trimble, and "Old Father" Lee as he was called. A short while after this, S. W. Womack was baptized by T. J. Shaw—"the man with the Book in his head." From the first the friendship of Womack and the white disciples was cordial, and he worshipped both early and late in life with them.

The line between the Disciples of Christ and the Church of Christ was not clearly drawn until the turn of this century. The differences were "fuzzy" and un-defined. Some men such as Alexander Campbell of Bethany, West Virginia, opposed instrumental music in worship, but not the missionary society. David Lipscomb had not made up his mind about the unscriptural nature of the missionary society until 1866. He took no decisive stand until 1874 against the use of the "organ" in Christian worship. Tolbert Fanning, a younger contemporary of Alexander Campbell and teacher of David Lipscomb, opposed both the "society" and the "organ." Not until around 1900 were the lines clearly drawn. This was largely due to the work of David Lipscomb and his associates. The disciples were generally said to belong to the Christian Church since the distinction of the church of Christ and Disciples of Christ did not exist until around the turn of this century. However, there were a few Negroes who identified themselves with the group around Tolbert Fanning and David Lipscomb. Womack was one of those. He complimented the *Gospel Advocate* in 1916, which he had been reading for fifty years. He wrote: "As far back as I can remember, in the days of the Lowries, Jones, Daniel Watkins, and William and Henry Lewis, and other colored

4

preachers of the churches of Christ, the columns of this paper have been open to all who wanted to write and make their reports."

By far and large, Negroes accepted religious unity reluctantly. Most slave holders in the South were Methodist and Baptists and their slaves were of the same religious persuasion. The plantation owners frowned upon the practice of leaving one church for another. They called it "jumping from limb to limb."

In the back country away from Nashville, the "music and society" issues bothered the Negro disciples not at all. They couldn't afford an organ or a piano, and anyhow couldn't play one. It was different in Nashville. Two fairly well established Christian Churches—the Lea Avenue and Gay Street churches were clearly identified with the Disciples of Christ. Campbell, and Womack and others who came in from the country identified with the Disciples of Christ since there was no other place to go.

Aleck Campbell, who was the first Negro Christian to withdraw from the Disciples of Christ because of "unscriptural innovations," added Womack and Bowser to his household of Christian disciples. From this modest beginning no larger than the "hands of three men," the restoration of New Testament Christianity among the Negro race was on its way.

How David Lipscomb entered the picture is not exactly known. By 1905 it was, however, clear that Campbell, Womack, and Bowser were sincere, capable, and could be trusted. The South Street College church of Christ where David Lipscomb served as an elder, and the Tenth Street church of Christ began supporting Campbell and Womack. Womack frequently mentioned in the *Gospel Advocate* the encouragement that he received from David Lipscomb.

A little known story in the life of David Lipscomb concerns his defense of the Negro as an individual and as a race: David Lipscomb was much too wise a man to dispute racial prejudice and too charitable to be blinded to justice and the demands of human decency. In 1907, sharp issue was taken with E. A. Elam in the *Gospel Advocate* because of a Negro girl reared in the Elam home. Elam and his wife carried her with them to Sunday worship. David Lipscomb wrote in Elam's defense: "I have never attended a church the Negroes did not attend. While they were slaves, we were glad for them to attend and become members of the church." David Lipscomb could not remember his own mother who had died in his infancy and his rearing for awhile was by a Negro woman. Negro children were among his playmates and he said, "I have always had the kindest feelings for them."

David Lipscomb regarded it to be the sacred duty of Christians to instruct the Negro and to encourage him to live a godly life. As long as he lived, Lipscomb took the lead in building meetinghouses for Negroes, and he preached for them in his younger days.

David Lipscomb had a blunt tongue and a sharp pen. And more than one person felt it in the *Gospel Advocate*. In 1867 David Lipscomb was holding a meeting near Trenton, Kentucky. The disciples had no meetinghouse and the Baptist Negroes kindly offered theirs. Lipscomb wrote: "Now some of you may be a little fearful that attending meeting in the Negro house will contaminate you, or you may be mistaken for Negroes. If there be such, they will be excused from attending; but all who are above suspicion may attend freely."

David Lipscomb wrote in 1901 what all men of good common sense had long known that "white men need not fear the curse of God because of the presence of the Negro. We are suffering it. This terrible crime and the constant dread of it is the penality we are paying for keeping the Negro in our midst ignorant and depraved, and using them for selfish ends."

Aleck Campbell was convinced around 1900 that the Disciples of Christ were engaging in unscriptural religious practices. His daughter, Alexine Campbell Page, stated that her father somehow came under the influence of David Lipscomb and the men associated with him in the *Gospel Advocate*. David Lipscomb had done his work so well through the *Gospel Advocate* that the U. S. Government religious census for 1906 listed the church of Christ and the Disciples of Christ as separate churches.

Aleck Campbell separated from the Lea Avenue Christian Church when guest preachers from the denominations filled the pulpit in the absence of Preston Taylor, the regular minister. The last time Campbell attended a service in the Lea Avenue building he challenged from the floor this and other religious innovations. The organist and the choir were directed to drown out his words. He left the services and never returned nor allowed any member of his family to go.

Campbell then retired to his home on Hardee Street with his wife, mother, sister, and daughter to worship God after the New

Testament pattern. He continued in this fashion for several months. Then Womack withdrew with his family from the Gay Street Christian Church to join hands with Campbell. This meant that Marshall and Minnie Keeble also joined with them. Keeble started on the "ground floor" with the older men and has played a leading role in the church among both races since that early day.

Aleck Campbell and S. W. Womack were unwilling just to "withdraw." They made a practice of going from house to house to convert others. The little church slowly grew. They purchased in 1906 a meetinghouse, the Fisk University Student Chapel, an old white frame building on Jackson Street. This was probably the first church home of loyal Negro disciples in Middle Tennessee, or perhaps anywhere around the turn of this century. It is a stubborn fact of history that from this handful of loyal Christians, New Testament Christianity among the Negroes got its first and most enduring impetus.

Aleck Campbell as a preacher of the gospel was all "fire and tow." Annie C. Tuggle described Campbell's preaching: "If God says in the Bible for me to jump through that wall, I'm going to jump, and I believe God will open that wall for me to go through." With great emotion he would declare that he was "standing on the Word of God." Whereupon he would throw his Bible to the floor and literally stand on it. He would then address his audience: "Now when you get home and start eating cornbread and sorghum molasses and drinking butter milk, and say, 'Now, I could have told that preacher so and so' "; Campbell would clinch his remark by saying, "if you've got something to say, say it now." B. C. Goodpasture as a boy remembers hearing Campbell preach. He was the first Negro preacher he had heard. Brother Goodpasture recalls that "Aleck Campbell was a 'top notch' preacher."

In 1906, C. A. Moore, a close associate of David Lipscomb and a trustee of the old Nashville Bible School, gave Campbell a tent to use in meeting work. That tent was set up from September to December on Horton Street, and fourteen persons were baptized. Today a fine congregation, the Twelfth Avenue South church of Christ grew out of that effort.

In August of 1906 Campbell started a meeting in a school house at Lawrenceburg, Tennessee. He so inflamed the sectarians that the doors were locked against him. Campbell convinced the county officials that he meant no harm and had been misrepresented. The doors of the school were consequently re-opened. A

7

favorite preaching place of Campbell in Nashville was down at the end of Broadway at the Cumberland River wharf where men came to loaf and to pick up jobs. Campbell was a good "street corner" preacher.

A good idea of Campbell's work is summarized in the *Gospel Advocate* for 1908. He conducted five tent meetings in Nashville and Smyrna, Tennessee, and Columbus, Mississippi. He conducted four meetings in private homes—two were in Blackton, Arkansas, and another in Turner, Arkansas. For the year, he received $327.82; of that amount $93.61 went for a tent and sawdust, moving the tent plus expenses for advertising cards, and street and railway fare.

From matters as small as a "mustard seed" great things happen. Womack proved to be as active and influential as Aleck Campbell. Womack conducted in 1904 a three weeks' meeting for the Jackson Street Mission. During the meeting, Joe McPherson, a member of the Jo Johnston church of Christ, preached five nights. McPherson was a white mail carrier. Several members from the Jo Johnston church attended the meeting with McPherson. This is seemingly an insignificant fact. But not so in the long haul of church history. Keeble said that he learned how to preach the gospel listening to Joe McPherson.

Womack was soon preaching far afield in Middle Tennessee. In the summer of 1905 Womack preached in Davidson, Putnam, and Wilson Counties. In late November, Womack re-traced his summer mission trail and found the new converts talking about "going into their winter quarters." He encouraged them to attend the church services regularly and to make their weekly contributions. And in 1906, Bowser with Womack, put up a tent on the corner of Park and Hamilton Streets in North Nashville. Each later year found Womack launching a little further out to preach the gospel. In 1908 he conducted forty-three religious services in Arkansas.

Womack was preaching in 1910 in the vicinities of Rogersville, Silver Run, and Mumford, Alabama. The Negro churches welcomed Womack and threw open their doors expecting to hear the usual sermons of the denominations. Womack echoed Paul in writing—"after the manner of men, I fought wild beasts at all these places." The doors of the church building were opened one night only to be closed the next. Womack won the respect and support of David Lipscomb until Lipscomb's death. It was his delight to visit with David Lipscomb and E. G. Sewell in the *Advocate* office where he often came for advice or instruction in Scriptures that were especially troublesome.

J. M. McCaleb wrote in 1911 some words in the *Gospel Advocate* that thrilled him as long as he lived: "Brother Womack is to the colored people what David Lipscomb is to the white people. He has built up a good name where he lives and is a benefactor to his race."

Campbell and Bowser also shared the confidence of David Lipscomb and his associates. Had it not been for their support, meager though it was, their modest successes would have been greatly curtailed. One of the earliest and most beloved friends of the Negro Christian was W. J. Hale, an illiterate white preacher. Hale had a remarkable memory of Bible verses. He preached mostly among the Negroes since the white people did not encourage him because of his lack of a formal education.

Alexine Campbell Page remembered that W. J. Hale often came to the Campbell home for someone to read the Bible to him. His power of memory was such that he could commit Scripture to memory sometimes on the first and always on the second reading. He would take his Bible and go out on the street to preach the gospel. Hale would say, "If you don't believe what I am preaching, take this Book, find it, and read it," all the while giving chapter and verse for the quotation. He would begin his service by singing a hymn and preaching. In his sermons he would say: "You can't go too high," then he would reach down and pick up a handful of dust and add, "for we are all made from this."

S. P. Pittman, longtime member of the faculty of David Lipscomb College, was another staunch friend of Womack, Campbell, and Bowser. He wrote to the *Gospel Advocate* recommending these men as good preachers able and worthy to perform a great work among their own people. One of the earliest and strongest apologists for the Negro and his cause was J. M. McCaleb, who spent several years in Japan as a missionary. He wrote in the *Gospel Advocate* decrying the narrow prejudices to downgrade the Negro and to show his incapacity to be civilized. He wrote that "the facts will continue to multiply against all such objections."

Three men stand out as the foremost champions of the Negro Christian in this century—David Lipscomb, Joe McPherson, and

A. M. Burton. David Lipscomb suffered a stroke in 1909 and steadily declined in health thereafter. Lipscomb started a "chain reaction" of substantial help to preach the gospel to the Negro race and to give the Negro the desire to secure a Christian education.

However important David Lipscomb's defense of the American Negro may be, Burton has exerted greater importance in the spread of the New Testament Christianity among the Negro race than any other single person. A. M. Burton needs no introduction to Christians in our time. He was born February 2, 1879, to J. Booker and Betty Laffety Burton near Hartsville, in Trousdale County, Tennessee. His childhood was spent with little educational opportunities. He attended a one room rural school for a total of twenty weeks. Their poor farm yielded the few necessities of life and none of the luxuries was enjoyed. Burton recalled near the close of his life that as a youth he was so poor he could not afford shoes and dress clothes to attend the rural neighborhood parties.

Burton left Trousdale County an eighteen year old boy to seek his fortune in the big city. He walked to Nashville leading a milch cow which he delivered to his grandmother. For almost a year, he worked as a day laborer on the excavation of the Chinese building during the preparations for the Tennessee Centennial celebration. He later worked as a carpenter's helper earning a dollar a day and managed to save half his wages.

A. M. Burton then entered the service of the Sun Life Insurance Company, and later worked as an agent for the Traders Mutual of Illinois. In 1903 with a thousand dollars, savings from his meager earnings, Burton persuaded Mrs. Helena Johnson, Dr. J. C. Franklin, and Guilford Dudley, Sr., and P. M. Estes, Sr. to supply the additional capital necessary to start the Life and Casualty Insurance Company. At the age of twenty-four, he was the youngest president of any American insurance company. That company today owns 413 million dollars in assets with three billion dollars of life insurance in force.

A. M. Burton said in the years of his greatest affluence, "I want to go back to God just like I was when I was a country boy and nothing in my hand." He and his wife, Lillie May Armstrong Burton whom he married a year after the insurance company started, have given some six million dollars to David Lipscomb College.

10

Burton's interest in the Negro started when he was selling industrial insurance to the poor working people in North Nashville. The world famous Fisk University is located in North Nashville in the Middle of a very large concentration of Negroes. Soon afterwards he organized his own insurance company.

Burton was attending a meeting in July of 1910 at the Highland Avenue church of Christ in Nashville where Charley M. Pullias was preaching. Pullias was born and grew up in Trousdale County. During that meeting Burton was baptized by Matthew Cayce. Joe McPherson and A. M. Burton formed a friendship that would have a far reaching influence on the church. McPherson enjoyed the respect of the members of the Jackson Street church because of his early interest in the work. Burton propositioned McPherson in 1914 to hold a meeting for the Jackson Street church. McPherson said, "What will the white people say if I do?" Brother Burton responded, "What will God say if you don't?" That's all it took. Burton had purchased his first Model T. Ford. He promised McPherson for his wages a ride out to his home near Madison, Tennessee, each evening in that "Model T."

Aleck Campbell assisted Joe McPherson during the meeting such as baptizing the converts and greeting the visitors. During that May meeting in 1914, Burton noticed a young man who was busy all over the place helping in every way he could. That person was none other than Marshall Keeble!

McPherson was a forceful preacher. He diagrammed his sermons plainly and simply on a chalkboard. Keeble took down every sermon that McPherson preached and learned how to diagram sermons. Keeble learned the art of preaching from that white mail carrier who walked the streets of Nashville by day and preached the gospel at night. Burton encouraged Keeble to preach the gospel not long afterwards.

When the meeting was going on, David Lipscomb was an old man and growing feebler by the day. But he was paying special attention to Burton. Lipscomb invited him to teach the auditorium class each Lord's day in the Nashville Bible School auditorium. "Aunt Mag" Lipscomb, David Lipscomb's wife, sat in Burton's class. Brother Burton knew she was a good student of the Bible and wondered why David Lipscomb had him to teach the auditorium class. There were other much better qualified teachers. "Wisdom is justified of her children," and David Lipscomb

11

was one of her favorites. Lipscomb was sizing up the church potentials of Burton. The Christian philantrophies of Andrew Mizel Burton since those days are also legend and a part of that story is told in this book.

It became apparent that the struggle to plant the cause of New Testament Christianity among the Negroes was firmly anchored in 1914. David Lipscomb's life would soon close. He had done his work carefully and remarkably well. S. W. Womack paid special attention to the death of David Lipscomb in 1917 when he wrote in the *Advocate* "It is our deepest regret to learn of the continued illness of our good brother of the *Gospel Advocate,* David Lipscomb." Following the death of David Lipscomb, S. W. Womack attended a service in December of 1917 in the Russell Street church in memory of David Lipscomb.

Unlike Elijah's spirit, Lipscomb's mantle fell on no one particular person. An equal portion fell on such men as Aleck Campbell, S. W. Womack, G. P. Bowser, and Marshall Keeble. They ably carried the word to their own race. A. M. Burton, H. Leo Boles, and others continued the life's work of Lipscomb among their race in the *Gospel Advocate* and the Nashville Bible School. And a great army of preachers went "everywhere preaching the word." The Christian men who manned the "Chariots of Israel" after the passing of David Lipscomb have since carried the cause of New Testament Christianity to every corner of the world. A diminutive Negro preacher living in North Nashville, who drove a huckster's wagon for a living, was destined to write a major chapter in church history.

Daughters of Major Horace Pinkney Keeble with Marshall Keeble
and Marshall Rose

13

CHAPTER II

The Huckster's Cry

Marshall Keeble was born December 7, 1878, in Rutherford County, Tennessee, in a small community located about two and a half miles from Murfreesboro on a toll pike. He was born in a log cabin that still stands. His father, Robert Keeble, was born into slavery. The Keeble surname which the slaves wore was one of the finest names of the aristocracy in the *ante bellum* South. The Keebles were among the early pioneers in Tennessee, and some of Tennessee's most distinguished citizens—past and present—wear the name proudly. John Bell Keeble served more than a generation ago as one of the great deans of the Vanderbilt University Law School. Marshall Keeble's grandfather was purchased by Major Horace Pinkney Keeble, a prominent lawyer in Murfreesboro.

During the Civil War, Marshall Keeble's grandfather traveled with Major Keeble as his personal valet. Major Keeble owned a small acreage on the Bradyville toll pike. The few servants he kept served the personal needs of the family and performed the chores about the farm. During the Civil War, the Yankees took over Major Keeble's home, and his wife went to live with Major Keeble's sister who resided in Murfreesboro. The story is told by the daughter of Major Keeble still living in Murfreesboro that Marshall Keeble's grandfather was shot while he was standing in the backyard of the Keeble home by a Union Soldier. However, Marshall Keeble remembers his grandfather. The Keeble servant—whoever he was—is not known to Marshall Keeble, and could not have been any relation to his grandfather who had been purchased by Major Keeble.

Robert and Mittie Keeble moved to Nashville, Tennessee, when Marshall was four years old. After the Civil War (Keeble's grandfather was also named Marshall and an uncle was named Marshall), the grandfather bought a small acreage from a white man by the name of Rube Head. Keeble remembers when he was a small boy the summer visits to his grandparents' home, and the grandmother petting her grandchildren, buttering their bread, and fixing them good things to eat. Especially the child Keeble en-

14

Keeble's birthplace

Keeble at twenty-two

M. Keeble

15

joyed riding the work horse or mule down to the pond or up from the fields. He was tickled to spend his summers with his grandparents out in the country.

Robert Keeble and his father could read and write. They were taught in the parlor of the house by either the "master or mistress" of the home. The cultural quality of the *ante bellum* Negro depended in a large measure on their owners. The gracious living of the Southern aristocracy was not without some benefits to them. One of the great secrets of Marshall Keeble's success has lain in his uncanny ability to win white people to his support. No preacher in the church of Christ—living or dead, a Bible scholar or a self taught man of either race—has won as many friends and kept them over a lifetime as has Marshall Keeble. A. M. Burton marvelled at this and asked Keeble in his last days—not how he made friends, but why he never lost a friend.

Marshall Keeble is equally popular among his own race. Some of the younger generation who can never know the world Marshall Keeble grew up in may think of him as an "old fashioned darky," but all who know this humble man should understand he never bowed to anyone but God. He is equally courteous to all. To say that he has suffered a great deal in life being a Negro would be mildly phrasing it. No man ever lived who was prouder of his own race than Marshall Keeble or brought greater credit to it. And he wants his race to be proud of him. They are!

Soon after Robert Keeble moved to Nashville, he began working for the city of Nashville and worked thirty years as a street cleaner driving a dump cart. The Keeble family lived on High Street (now Sixth Avenue North). Marshall Keeble tells no "hard luck" story of bitter poverty. Robert Keeble made a good living for his family and was devoted to them. The philosophy of Marshall Keeble was formed early in life as he witnessed the firm religious convictions of his parents. They set a high store on personal character and respected the fruits of hard labor.

Marshall Keeble remembers first attending church services with his mother and father in a building owned by a doctor on North Spruce Street (now Eighth Avenue North). The small band was a split that had pulled out of the Gay Street Christian Church. Preston Taylor was their preacher who led the group out of the Gay Street Church. Robert Keeble was assistant minister to Taylor. Preston Taylor's chief claim to fame lies in the fact that he was the first licensed Negro undertaker in Nashville; and

16

as the story goes, the first one in the South. The small church finally located on Lea Avenue in a church building of their own. Marshall Keeble remembers his father with deep affection. When the snow lay deep and he was a small boy, his father would carry him on his back to church and school. Marshall Keeble was baptized by Preston Taylor in the Gay Street Christian church when Keeble was fourteen years old.

Marshall Keeble never went beyond the seventh grade. His father bought a house, and Marshall had to go to work to help pay for the home. His first two years of schooling were in the Bellview School located on Summer Street (now Fifth Avenue North). Next he attended Knowles School located between Jackson and Hamilton Street (now Herman Street) until he finished the seventh grade. When asked how he ranked in his class at school, Keeble quickly responded—"At the head of his class"; and Keeble has been at the head of his class ever since. There is no cause to lament Keeble's lack of a formal education. Shakespeare knew little Latin and less Greek. As Alexander Campbell—the Bethany preacher—said, "Raccoon John Smith was the only preacher he ever knew that a formal education would have ruined." It is doubted that Keeble's preaching ability would have been improved had he gone to college.

Keeble's first regular job was in a bucket factory where he worked six ten-hour days a week earning forty-cents hourly wages. His task was carrying poplar and cedar staves to the workmen who were making wooden tubs, churns, and buckets that were shipped out by the car loads. Tin buckets had not yet come of age.

Marshall Keeble's next job when he was eighteen years of age was in a soap factory owned by the Cassity Coal Company. He operated a soap press powered with a foot pedal and fed by hand. Keeble said he was mighty good on that machine and he got "too professional"; and while laughing and joking once too often with other employees, in a careless moment, he severed the first joint of his right index finger. Keeble said he was often asked how he lost that finger. Sometimes the question was thought to embarrass him since he could have gotten "that finger shot off in a crap game." When Keeble explained, he said it always got him honor.

Keeble remembers the brand names of the soap—Tokyo, Clairmax, and Cracker Jack. He said they were shaped up differently with a variety of colors and perfumes. Some users swore by one brand and some by another. Keeble said, "It was the same soap."

One of the decisive influences in the life of Marshall Keeble was his marriage to Minnie Womack, daughter of S. W. Womack. Keeble was both baptized and married into the Christian Church. Robert Keeble's home was next door to the Womacks. This is how Keeble got acquainted with the family.

Minnie Womack was a graduate of the high school department of Fisk University when the internationally famed Milo Cravat was the white president of Fisk University. Keeble married Minnie Womack when he was eighteen, and lived for a while in the Womack home. Those were the days when Keeble worked for a living in the soap factory. Keeble never tires of repeating that marrying into the Womack family was one of the great blessings of his life. Womack was the epitome of southern courtesy and possessed with a gentleness that pleased white people. He was held in high esteem by them. In 1912 when he was holding a two night meeting at Cook Place near Cookeville, Tennessee, in the white meetinghouse; they came out in large numbers to hear him. Marshall Keeble learned early in life from his father and Womack how to get along with the white Southerner who exercised throughout the South both power and influence.

Minnie Keeble was a good wife and mother and her superior education was used to Keeble's advantage. Annie C. Tuggle said—"She was kind of fiery and high tempered, but she was a devout and active Christian." Keeble said she criticized his English or whatever about his preaching that needed special attention. Keeble added sometimes he got tired of too much criticism so often. Keeble would complain, "I don't think I said that." Minnie Keeble had a quick tongue to praise or to reprimand and she would answer Keeble—"Yes, you did say it." That ended the matter. Even after the death of Minnie Keeble at the age of fifty-three, and that was forty-five years ago, he still speaks of her as "being my best teacher." Keeble said Minnie tried to make a "Fiskite" out of him correcting his language.

Marshall and Minnie Keeble were the parents of five children. Two died in their infancy. Clarence, ten at the time, met a sudden death when he was playing in front of the Keeble home. He touched an exposed high voltage wire on a utility pole. Keeble said his wife never seemed to be very well after that great sorrow. Beatrice Elnora died in November, 1935, just a short while after

18

her mother's passing. The only surviving child was Robert Keeble who died in 1964. Marshall Keeble has outlived all of his relatives and immediate family. Two daughters of Elnora are living and two grandchildren. Marshall Keeble had a brother, Peter, also a resident of Nashville, who worked for the L & N Railroad. Peter Keeble died in his seventies. Two other brothers and a sister died in their infancy. George Keeble, an uncle of Marshall Keeble, worked about fifty years for Vanderbilt University. Both brother and uncle were members of the church of Christ.

Keeble has been a fast moving man all his life. After the "soap factory" days Keeble went into business for himself. He opened a small grocery store on Hamilton Street largely run by Minnie. He purchased a huckster's wagon, and his route was down Hayes Street and West End Avenue which was then an elite section of Nashville. Keeble said the white people enjoyed buying their produce from him and waited for his wagon and scolded him when he was late. Keeble had his wagon painted to a high gloss and always spotlessly clean. His fine black horse was well groomed and shining. The leather harness was polished and the brass ornaments were gleaming. Keeble would go down to the farmer's market about three or four in the morning and load his wagon down with choice produce. Dressed in a white apron Keeble sang out in his rich baritone voice his tomatoes or potatoes or whatever vegetables were in season. Keeble opened a second store on Jefferson Street operated by his wife; and his sister-in-law, Philistia Womack, ran the Hamilton Street store.

Keeble changed his pattern with the coming of winter. He bought wood by the car load and kept a blind man for several years cutting wood every day with a buck saw. Few Negroes then owned coal stoves. Keeble hauled wood and coal in his huckster's wagon over chosen streets. Keeble stated the day never got too cold for him to go dressed in "high top" boots driving his sure-footed well-shod horse. Keeble said he "had always been a hustler," and rain, snow, or whatever stopped most men just slowed him down a little.

Keeble said at one time the city council passed an ordinance because of pressure from grocery men forbidding the hucksters to cry their produce on the street. One day he forgot and started "hollering" his produce going down West End Avenue. Suddenly a policeman appeared from a side street sternly reprimanding him.

19

Keeble knew he was about to be arrested. Never at a loss to think quickly and come up with the appropriate words, he explained,

"Excuse me Cap, I've been doing this so long I clean forgot." Keeble said that word "cap" brought a big smile to the officer's face and saved the day.

He demanded to know the owner of the wagon and Marshall responded, "It belongs to Mr. Keeble."

The white Keebles of Nashville were then living in the current fame of John Bell Keeble, Dean of the Vanderbilt Law School.

The policeman told Keeble, "Well, you tell him the next time I catch you hollering out here on the street, I'm going to make him pay a fine."

Keeble said that quick thinking saved him a five or ten dollar fine. Keeble and Minnie had a good laugh over "Mr. Keeble's wagon" and how fortunate it was for him that the officer failed to ask for the house address of "Mr. Keeble," who was living on Jefferson Street.

Keeble was always trying to make a dollar in the "huckster" days and they came slow and hard. On holidays when all businesses were closed down and especially on bitter cold days when everyone was at home, he would be out peddling coal. One of his early friends was Matthew C. Cayce who owned the Cayce Transport and Coal Company. Keeble would drive his wagon into the closed yard to load coal with Cayce's permission.

Two policemen stopped and charged Keeble, "Don't you know this coal yard is closed?"

Keeble answered, "Mr. Cayce told me to come in and load up my wagon."

With something less than politeness, one officer said, "He hasn't told you any such thing. Get down off that wagon!"

Keeble advised the officer, "I know his telephone number; just tell him who told you to call."

The officer said, "I'll get his number. You wait right here and don't drive off." Keeble has always been patient with the Caucasian as well as the Negro, so he waited first on one foot and then on the other.

The officer returned and gruffly said, "Go ahead"; and Keeble added, "He didn't say pardon me or nothing, and he had almost cussed me."

Marshall Keeble grew up respecting labor and the joy of a job well done. His great boyhood idol was Booker T. Washington. Keeble heard the immortal Booker T. Washington each time he came to Nashville always speaking to overflow crowds in the Sam Jones Tabernacle that for many years now has been the home of the world-famed "Grand Ole Opry." Keeble said you got there to hear the great Negro educator thirty minutes ahead of time if you hoped to get a seat or even get in. Keeble knew *Up From Slavery* from lid to lid. He said there were some things he learned from Booker T. Washington he couldn't learn from the Bible. By that Keeble meant he learned to respect his race, to hold a high opinion of himself, and especially how to get along with white people. The freed Southern Negro had known only back-breaking toil, and he had little respect for hard labor after freedom came. Booker T. Washington respected labor and knew the Negro's first step upward had to be through learning skilled trades. While attending Hampton Institute, Washington saw his white benefactors at the school doing the most menial labor scrubbing and washing to keep every "nook and cranny" spotless clean. Keeble said: "He was my idol—all he lacked was being a Christian." Keeble also learned how Booker T. Washington raised money for his school from white people. And Keeble years later would follow suit in raising money for the Nashville Christian Institute.

Keeble started preaching some time after the turn of this century. Just when he started preaching is not known and Keeble doesn't remember. But after Campbell and Womack pulled out of the Christian Church, Keeble was with them. A lack of words is not a Keeble failing, and he probably became a preacher by preaching all along.

Any how he was preaching early in this century. Womack thought it worth mentioning to report in the *Advocate* that M. Keeble preached for a small band of disciples at the Dozier School house on the third Lord's day in May, 1908. The steps of Marshall Keeble from that day until this may be certainly traced, and the pen or typewriter has not yet been invented, nor the man born that can actually tell the true stories of this incredible little dark-skinned man whose words and deeds thread through legions of tales that have grown around him. Fortunately most of the biographical information is recorded in the *Gospel Advocate* which Keeble first discovered when he married into the Womack household.

21

By 1910 Marshall Keeble was not exactly a young man. But he was trying out his "preaching legs" and standing pretty well. His mother-in-law often said in those days to her husband—"as long as heaven is happy, Marshall will never make a preacher." Keeble laughs while he tells this story adding "that according to her prediction that meant forever." In her declining years her son-in-law was her beloved preacher. When Keeble would be in town "Aunt Sally" Womack would demand that Marshall speak this morning at the Jackson Street church of Christ so she could hear her "favorite preacher."

Marshall Keeble continued to support his family through hard labor after he entered the ministry. When he came home from his meetings, he would straighten out all the "odds and ends" that had accumulated during his absence. Keeble always had to figure close to meet his financial obligations, and it was not until the 1920's when he came to the attention of the leading members of the church that life became easier. Minnie was a good manager, and Keeble would leave home with complete assurance that she would be equal to her responsibilities. Keeble made the momentous decision of his life in 1914 when he decided to give up all and preach the gospel the rest of his life. Fifty-four years have now passed. Keeble is eighty-nine years old. He still commands great audiences with the simple announcement that "Marshall Keeble will speak tonight" and he is still baptizing people.

CHAPTER III

School Days At Silver Point

One of the most stirring and courageous chapters in the Restoration of New Testament Christianity centers in the struggles of a handful of Negro Christians to found a school shortly after the turn of this century similar to David Lipscomb's old Nashville Bible School. Those were the days when Booker T. Washington was engaging in one of America's great heroic epics to elevate the southern Negro through education in Tuskegee, Alabama.

The average white church member and practically all Negro disciples today know about Marshall Keeble's Nashville Christian Institute and Southwestern—a junior college for Negroes in Terrell, Texas. The story of Christian education among Negroes actually begins in the early days of this century when Aleck Campbell, S. W. Womack and G. P. Bowser organized a grade school in the Jackson Street Mission where the Bible would be taught daily.

In conversations with David Lipscomb, Campbell, Womack and Bowser were encouraged by Lipscomb to start a Bible School on their own to see what they could do with it. Lipscomb promised them as soon as the debt was cleared on the Nashville Bible School he would help them all he could and would interest others to help. With this encouragement, the three men organized a little elementary school in the Jackson Street church.

It was in 1905 that Campbell, Womack, Bowser, and other interested people entered into discussions to start a school of their own like the Nashville Bible School. A meeting was called at the Jackson Street church to this end. An agenda was prepared calling for discussions on four points:—(1) Evangelistic and Mission Work; (2) Innovations in the Work; (3) Financial Conditions of the Church; (4) The Constitution (of the school).

Hope ran high for the success of such a school among the members of the Jackson Street church. Charles W. Smith, who was connected with the Womack family, made the opening address to a packed house on the subject—"The Need of a School Among the Colored People." Smith was a student in Fisk University. Arrangements were made during the meeting to secure a tent for evangelistic work in the following year. In the course of the meeting $720.00 was subscribed and turned over to the school directors who were authorized to use the money as they deemed best.

On October 8, 1907, Bowser and Womack opened the Jackson Street School. The enrollment reached seventeen that first year. The school was operated under the auspices of the colored disciples and was supported principally by their donations with some assistance from the church at Sparta, Tennessee, and the Jo Johnston church in Nashville. The daughter of Marshall and Minnie Keeble, Elnora, gave up a Fisk University scholarship to attend the new school. Keeble said, "I took her out of Fisk to recognize our school." In much the same fashion that David Lipscomb had a hand in about everything that pertained to the crucial decisions that shaped the course of Restoration history in his lifetime, Keeble has exerted a similar influence on the growth of the New Testament church among members of his race.

G. P. Bowser and S. W. Womack labored hard to build a school on Jackson Street. Although Womack had taught school around Lynchburg, Tennessee, he gave all his time to preaching after moving to Nashville. History will not record the name of Bowser for any great school he founded, but he rightfully deserves to be described as the "Father of Christian Education" among the Negro Christians. He worked most of his life single handedly to establish a loyal Christian school among his people. In one sense Bowser's efforts to start a Christian College was finally realized in the establishing of Southwestern Christian College in Terrell, Texas.

It was the responsibility of Bowser to manage the new school with one assistant. Womack was unfailing in his support of Bowser's school efforts and wrote often about the school in the *Gospel Advocate*. When Bowser would be away from the school, Womack would "pinch hit" for him.

The school did not stay long in Nashville. In 1909 the institution was moved to Silver Point, Tennessee. It was believed that the cost of maintaining the school at Silver Point would be less in a rural setting and food could be raised for students at little cost. Silver Point was an isolated settlement. Before a school site was purchased in Silver Point, a meeting was called in the Old Putnam County School building. The public school then in use was about three miles from the site. This meeting was called by S. W. Womack, Aleck Campbell, Henry Clay, Sam David, Marshall Keeble,

24

and G. P. Bowser. The meeting was to acquaint the Negro community about the plans for a Negro school. G. P. Bowser spoke during the meeting which was well attended. Bowser was appointed a teacher by the Putnam County School Board. The county allowed them to use their one room school house until the new school was built. A school site was purchased at Silver Point in 1909 for $250.00, and a two-story frame structure was erected at the cost of $600.00. Two teachers were employed and their salaries never exceeded $50.00 a month. The school advertised its program formally in the Negro religious publication *The Christian Echo*:

Tuition:	Model, 50¢; Grammar, 75¢; Normal, $1.00 Board and Lodging, $6.00.
Sustenance:	This school is sustained by tuitions and donations. This accords everyone the privilege of helping a laudable movement.
Course of Study:	The school is designed to meet the requirements of a Normal Institution with the Bible taught as a text book.
Location:	By action of the trustees and brethren assembled in Nashville, October 13-15, the school was moved from Nashville to Silver Point, seventy-five miles east on the Tennessee Central Railroad.

Actually the school at Silver Point would be described today as an elementary and high school. G. P. Bowser was graduated from Walden University in Nashville, Tennessee. The university was operated by the Methodist Church. It was not difficult to imagine the formidable challenges that two teachers faced attempting such a task. But they tried and their struggles were heroic.

In 1910 Womack spent two weeks with Bowser at Silver Point. Womack's daughter, Philistia, was teaching with Bowser at that time. Womack and Campbell assisted Bowser in whatever way they could to make a go of the little school. A long, long look from the present back to these days discloses the futility of their dreams. Outside of David Lipscomb, A. M. Burton, S. P. Pittman, and a few others, little interest and less money came from those who could have helped. Only a few white people knew about the school at Silver Point. The few that did never gave much. The Negroes were generally poor and could help only a little.

As early as 1912 A. M. Burton was helping with the support of the Silver Point school. His new insurance company was prospering. David Lipscomb began to pay special attention to Burton and gradually involved him in the affairs of the church.

Another person deserving special attention in connection with the Silver Point school is Annie C. Tuggle. She was reared near Memphis, Tennessee, and came under the influence of Aleck Campbell and G. P. Bowser. She became interested in the school in 1913, and served first as a teacher and later as a solicitor. Alexine Campbell Page, daughter of Aleck Campbell, was also one of Bowser's teachers. The talented T. H. Busby taught music in the school.

Annie C. Tuggle told of her train ride from Nashville to Silver Point with Bowser. He cautioned her not to expect too much. She was disappointed when she saw the pitiful two-story frame building which housed the school on the first floor and the boarding dormitory for students on the second floor. The little furniture was of the poorest quality; and during the winter, the building was heated by stoves with the stove pipes sticking through the windows. Bowser tried where men of less faith would have never started.

There is an interesting side story in the Silver Point School that developed in 1915. In a meeting of the board of trustees of the Putnam County Normal and Industrial School (the Silver Point school) for Colored People, Aleck Campbell confessed a fault that the trustees unwittingly committed. To show their disapproval of the innovations in Christian worship and practices (they had the Christian Church particularly in mind), the board made a formal declaration registering their feelings. A. M. Burton told them that what they had done actually amounted to their writing a creed and the Bible already condemned all unscriptural practices. Aleck Campbell wrote the following statement for the *Gospel Advocate*:

ALEXANDER CAMPBELL MAKES ACKNOWLEDGEMENT

To the *Gospel Advocate*: In the *Gospel Advocate* of October 29, 1914, there appears a report of a meeting of the trustees of the Putnam County Normal and Industrial School for colored people.

After a careful consideration and mature deliberation upon my part, I have become convinced that the act of authorizing our names to be placed on the minutes saying that we will not fellowship certain preachers was denominational in its nature, and, though, I did not so consider it at the time, equivalent to writing a creed to govern the conduct or conscience of other men.

Believing it to be preeminently proper to acknowledge our faults and to correct any evil that we may have done, I take this opportunity, as far as I am individually concerned, to rescind this action; and in so much as quite a good deal has been written in the *Advocate* concerning this matter, I will thank you to allow space for this statement.   ALEXANDER CAMPBELL

A determined campaign was carried on in 1916 to make something of the Negro school. Annie C. Tuggle told of a conversation she had with David Lipscomb about the school. She rode the street car out to his farm and was cordially invited into Lipscomb's home. Annie C. Tuggle stated her mission and remembers that David Lipscomb said these words, "Young lady, I don't have any money, but I have friends who do. And I am going to see to it that you can have a school where the Bible will be taught daily."

David Lipscomb's Nashville Bible School was prospering under the presidency of H. Leo Boles. One of the last acts in the life of David Lipscomb was to solicit the help of A. M. Burton to make a survey of the Silver Point school facilities and to make recommendations for increased services of the institution.

From an initial enrollment of nine when the school first opened on Jackson Street, the enrollment at the end of the school year in the spring of 1915 was fifty-seven. The following year was actually the highest point the little school ever reached.

There were reasons for the optimism in 1916. The school had attracted very little attention outside of David Lipscomb and a small circle of friends. In 1916 A. M. Burton was commissioned by David Lipscomb to go to Silver Point and to make a survey for the future propsects of the school. Burton was accompanied by J. S. Hammond, another interested friend, to Silver Point. They spent one day, January 5, looking over the community and the school grounds. About two hundred white and Negro families lived within a two mile radius of the railroad station.

Burton reported to David Lipscomb that the property of the Bible school consisted of eight acres of poor land about one mile from the station. A residence had been bought for Bowser in addition to the frame Chapel building in very bad repair. Both buildings were worth about $1000.00. The school had nine boarding students at the time.

A. M. Burton mentioned a small printing press at the school (owned by G. P. Bowser), and that the faculty and students were issuing at small cost a monthly paper—*The Christian Echo.* Burton advised Lipscomb there was no market for the little farm produce that the students grew except for their own use.

27

The name of Henry H. Clay was mentioned by Burton. Clay was a blacksmith who built wagons from the ground up with the help of school boys. Henry Clay was an ex-slave and a Union soldier. He was prosperous and held in high regard by the white people of the community. He gave generously of his time and little money to the school. He was possessed with a great store of common sense and a gentle heart to help raise up his race. Henry Clay had a good knowledge of the Bible and wanted it taught to his race. Alexine Campbell Page described Henry Clay as a heavy set, dark man, with red eyes. "He was an old fashioned fellow and a sincere worker for the church."

As a result of Burton's visit, new lots were purchased at a cost of $275.00. A commodious brick chapel building to house the school was erected on the site. The material of the old chapel building was utilized to build a four room frame house for boarding girls. A. M. Burton shipped brick, lime and cement to Silver Point by the carload. The total cost of the materials came to $400.00. P. H. Black, a Nashville bricklayer, who, Brother Burton complimented as the best in the trade, laid the brick free of charge. He also helped build the first building at Silver Point. His helper was a teen-age boy, Robert Campbell, the son of Aleck Campbell. Robert Campbell was a member of the Jefferson Street church of Christ, a Nashville undertaker, and a long time board member of the Nashville Christian Institute.

The Silver Point School was then organized under a board of trustees composed of A. M. Burton, S. P. Pittman, J. S. Hammond, O. P. Barry, Alexander Campbell, S. W. Womack, P. H. Black, Henry Clay, and Marshall Keeble. A. M. Burton served as Treasurer. Annie C. Tuggle became an official solicitor for the school. She wrote often to the *Gospel Advocate* and worked hard for the support of the school. Such support that came was meager.

Robert Burns observed that the best laid plans of mice and men often go "haywire." In spite of all the effort put forth at Silver Point, the school was doomed. In the year of its seeming re-birth, David Lipscomb died. Though the Nashville Bible School faced stern tests, its security was well established by the time of Lipscomb's passing.

Two major problems faced the Silver Point school from the word "go" and finally closed it down—to attract a student body to the remote mountain region and to sustain it financially. The school gradually withered away. Following the first world war, Henry H. Clay said brave words concerning new efforts being made by friends of the school including "Aunt Mag," David Lipscomb's widow: "This move means success or no school for the colored disciples. What shall it be? What you do may decide the matter. We can, we must, we shall succeed."

Two years later the school closed its doors. The chapel building still serves as the meetinghouse for the Negro disciples at Silver Point. It was never as a matter of too late—just too little. The Negro Christians had no money to build a school, and the white disciples were desperately struggling to build schools of their own. They too were generally poor.

It would be a serious error to think the school at Silver Point met an ignominious end. The school was a sincere expression of the Negro race to want something better than they had ever known—a Christian school for their children. Their faith was great enough to move mountains. The grandchildren of these pioneers are today enjoying the finest training that Christian colleges and schools can afford them.

Womack announced in the *Gospel Advocate* that plans were being made to faze out the school at Silver Point at the end of the school year 1919-1920. H. D. Gilbert finished out the last school term. And so the dream to start an institution like the Nashville Bible School ended temporarily. The Negro disciples waited another twenty years before they had a school of their own—The Nashville Christian Institute. A M. Burton did not give up so easily for a Negro Bible school where they could also learn some useful trade. Burton purchased the old Florence Crittenton Home for unwed mothers in South Nashville. The home was moved to a new location. Burton described the plans for the new school in both the *Gospel Advocate,* and in a letter he wrote to A. B. Lipscomb.

Dear Brother Lipscomb:
    In accordance with my promise I shall try to tell you something of the proposed Bible School for Negroes in Nashville.
    The property I recently purchased, formerly the Florence Crittenton Home, will be used for this purpose. It is located on Ewing Avenue in the midst of the largest Negro settlement in Nashville, and is well fitted for the purpose. There are about thirty-five bedrooms, large halls for Chapel and recitations, commodious dining room, laundry, kitchen, etc. The heating plant warms all the rooms and furnishes hot water.
    The purpose of the school is to train colored boys and girls to be self-respecting and self-supporting by becoming true Christians. The Bible will be taught daily as a part of the school curriculum, and each student will be

required to do a certain amount of manual labor in the school or in outside homes. All the duties of the school will be performed by students, thus giving them the benefit of experience and at the same time keeping down the expense of operation.

I have personally bought the building and will donate its use to the Negro Bible School, and will appreciate the help of the brotherhood in fitting up the different rooms. For this purpose we can use furniture no longer needed in our homes. Clothing outgrown or out of style will also be very acceptable and can be worked over at the school and used to good purpose. A list of articles needed is enclosed, being so arranged that the smallest child can contribute "something" to this worthy cause.

Russell Street is the first congregation before which I wish to place the needs of the school. I trust that response will be such that we can feel a pride in printing same in the school paper as a pattern and example to others.

In this school work we will try as far as we can to do the full work of the church among the Negroes, according to strict Bible teaching. Having established a congregation, we will not only try to make the Bible the standard by which the members are guided personally, but extend the influence of the school in other ways, with members to visit widows and orphans in their affliction as well as minister to those sick and in prison. In the school we will have a spare bed for the stranger who would spend the night.

Hoping you will be moved in your hearts to make a liberal response to this appeal, I am

Yours in Christ,
A. M. BURTON

It was named the Southern Practical Institute. Plans were made to open the school January 5, 1920, with prospects of some forty or fifty students.

Burton was impressed with a large training school for young Negroes in the neighborhood conducted by the Catholic Church where tuition was almost nothing. A. M. Burton in expressing his interest in the new school said that he had heard on the previous Wednesday evening one of the best sermons he had heard in years preached by a sixteen year old Negro, Nathan Hogan. Brother Burton had in mind R. N. Hogan. G. P. Bowser brought young Hogan to Silver Point from Blackton, Arkansas, and kept him in his home four years. The young boy traveled with Bowser on preaching appointments and learned how to preach under Bowser's supervision. R. N. Hogan for many years has been one of the foremost evangelists among the churches of Christ.

The Southern Practical Institute in South Nashville was born and died in the space of six weeks. G. P. Bowser, assisted by Misses Willie D. Wall and Annie C. Tuggle, started the school. There are conflicting statements as to why the school failed, but it did. A. M. Burton dropped out of the picture to promote a Christian school among the Negro race. Along about this time Burton was made a member of the Board of Directors of David

Lipscomb College, and his contributions to Christian education is one of the epic stories of our time.

While the name of G. P. Bowser will not be recorded as a great Southern Negro educator, a member of the Negro race was never more determined than he to establish a Christian school among his people. When the school faded away at Silver Point and the school in south Nashville failed before it started, Bowser moved to Louisville, Kentucky, to preach the gospel. He next made an attempt to start a school in Detroit, Michigan, that operated a short while. Bowser started and operated for eight years the Bowser Christian Institute in Fort Smith, Arkansas, where he moved from Detroit.

To start and sustain a Christian school for Negroes was the crowning obsession of Bowser's life. He moved next to Fort Worth, Texas, to organize another school. Though G. P. Bowser never headed a school that long endured, he sowed the seed and desire in the hearts of the Negro Christians to secure a Christian education that is strongly persevering today.

G. P. Bowser died March 23, 1950, but the ambition to found a school like the Nashville Bible School did not end with Bowser's passing. It was through his efforts to start schools in Louisville, Detroit, Fort Smith, and Fort Worth that birth was given to the Nashville Christian Institute and Southwestern in Terrell, Texas.

A. M. Burton kept alive in his own mind the desire to create a school especially designed to train preachers like Marshall Keeble. He wrote Keeble a letter dated September 19, 1924.

Dear Brother Keeble:

Your letter of the 16th is received. Also I received your other letter in regard to the fine work near Paducah.

I am so glad to learn that you have been able to establish a church there and create so much interest.

It is indeed interesting to calculate just what we could do if we had seventy-five or one hundred colored preachers like you. It may be that some time this winter we can start a night school, or Bible class, to meet once or twice a week and develop more of the younger colored people into preachers.

I mailed to your home address a few days ago a letter received from a brother down in Mississippi wanting you to hold a meeting for them.

I am always glad to hear from you as nothing is more inspiring to learn of people being baptized into the name of the Father, Son, and Holy Spirit, also to hear that new congregations are being established.

Yours fraternally,
A. M. BURTON

Annie C. Tuggle visited back at Silver Point in 1925 and heard old Henry Clay speak during the worship service. And she wrote for the *Gospel Advocate*—"A contribution was taken for the unborn Nashville Christian Institute." But this is another story that will be told in another place.

H. B. Watkins, a Negro preacher, held in 1939 a meeting at Silver Point. He wrote words that must have brought back poignant memories—"On August 18, I closed a very good meeting at Silver Point, Tennessee, in the old brick building where G. P. Bowser began his work long long ago."

It is true Keeble's Nashville Christian Institute did not grow out of Silver Point, but it is equally true that the great life of Keeble is deeply rooted in the efforts of Aleck Campbell, S. W. Womack, and G. P. Bowser. To each he owes a great debt of gratitude, and Keeble is generous to acknowledge that he is a great debtor to these benefactors.

CHAPTER IV

The Jackson Street David

When the church on Jackson Street turned fourteen years old, Marshall Keeble made up his mind to give all his life to evangelizing. He sold his huckster's wagon, but Minnie continued to run the store on Jefferson Street. When Keeble returned home from his meetings, he would help in the store or pick up a bucksaw and begin cutting firewood to peddle in the neighborhood. Keeble and his wife continued to operate the grocery store a good long while after Keeble was preaching full time to help support their growing family.

Finally the word got through to the white people, as an elderly Negro said in Keeble's Valdosta, Georgia, meeting that "a great prophet has appeared in our midst." Keeble no longer had to preach the gospel by working part time. At this late day in Keeble's life, no one needs to guess his feelings for white people, They have been his friends too long for him to doubt their sincerity. The days came when threats "to tar and feather" him meant nothing because his white Christian friends stood by his side.

When Keeble started going out of town to preach the gospel, he got some old worn out and mildewed suitcases of S. W. Womack out from under the house. He cleaned and polished them, and fastened the packed suitcase securely with pieces of bright hay baling wire. Then he hurried to Union Station to catch the Dixie Flyer or whatever train that was heading out in the direction he was going.

Keeble was soon preaching all over the South. What a figure the "Jackson Street David" cut! When he came into town, he would be wearing a derby hat and a frock-tailed coat. Bubbling over with good humor, he radiated joy wherever he went. A favorite preaching time was on Saturdays. This was the day when all the Negroes in great numbers came in from the countryside. Keeble said the sidewalks were so full a person had to get out in the street to go anywhere.

Keeble would soon be standing on a curb stone, the back-end of a wagon, or on top of a bale of cotton preaching the gospel. And the way Keeble preached would have made Peter and Paul sit up and take instant notice. He put his derby hat in a convenient spot, and it would be flooded with pennies, nickels, dimes, and occasional quarters.

As Keeble ranged over Tennessee and adjacent states preaching the gospel, he remembers the cabins the Negroes lived in. Some were clapboard houses and others built with logs. Few had glass windows—just boards fastened to hinges that could be closed against the snow and rain. Many a night Keeble went to bed in the loft deep down in a feather bed with quilts pulled high over his head. The next morning he could reach out and take up a handful of snow that had sifted in through the cracks. Those were happy occasions! After services they would sit around the fire place with sweet potatoes roasting in the hot ashes and enjoy themselves. Keeble happily remembers those days.

Although the first time Keeble preached a sermon is unknown, he was engaged in church work in the Jackson Street Mission from the start. He was appointed treasurer of the church. That speaks well for any man. Whatever his first preaching efforts were like may be surmised from his mother-in-law who told S. W. Womack he was wasting his time: "Marshall's not preaching material, and there's no use for him to waste his time or the people's time. A preacher has to be a preacher. Marshall's not a preacher."

Keeble was an apt pupil and he learned his lessons well. Aleck Campbell was one of his first and best teachers. Keeble said no man labored as hard and earnestly as Campbell always in the face of heart breaking hindrances. In Keeble's early preaching days, Campbell carried Keeble with him into Jackson County to preach. Many members of the Jefferson and Jackson Street churches trace their conversions to those occasions.

On one of those preaching trips an old lady rose to dispute with Campbell and said that the "Scripture" was not in her Bible, and Campbell was invited to her house to see for himself. So the next day Campbell and Keeble drove out in a farm wagon to her gate. Campbell was extremely courteous. After the usual pleasantries he took her Bible and flipped to the place and back again—but it was not there. Then she told Campbell, "That Scripture was bothering my religion and I clipped it out." Later in a big meeting while Campbell was preaching hard and wet with perspiration, he would say, "It's in your Bible if you haven't clipped it out." Keeble said when Campbell got through preaching the Bible "nothing was standing but the house."

Keeble does remember his first meeting at Center Star near Centerville, Tennessee. He baptized twenty-five people in Blue Buck Pond. Keeble took great heart from this experience. This was one of the decisive factors that encouraged him to spend his life preaching the gospel. Many years later when Keeble became famous, his friends were afraid the compliments would spoil him. T. Q. Martin summed it up when he said, "Marshall Keeble is too intelligent a man for compliments to spoil him."

Keeble had many great teachers. But Campbell and Womack took their first turns in training him. Keeble said Campbell was "fiery and passionate" in his preaching and Womack was "cool and slow in getting to a point." Keeble said—"I got the best from both." Years afterwards Keeble remarked, "Campbell and Womack fired me up and left here!"

The year Keeble made up his mind to preach full-time, Joe McPherson and A. M. Burton conducted the famed Jackson Street meeting. Two years later he wrote, "I find no time to rest in the work. I am busy every day somewhere preaching the gospel, for my people certainly need it." For many years now, Keeble is flooded with invitations to preach. Keeble goes where in his best judgment he can do the most good. No man could be less interested in money for personal uses. Keeble has never gone for "hand outs." Many of his Christian friends have great wealth, and stand instantly ready to supply any personal needs of his.

Marshall Keeble remembers the kind of support he got in those early days. He would carry home pigs, hams and rabbits in a tow sack. All the baggage masters up and down the line came to know and love the "Happy Little Warrior" and often carried his load for free. Sometimes he got a gallon of molasses, and $2.00 was a big collection. There were "stops" up and down the railroad where Keeble's friends carried him. Many a delighted conductor who had not seen Keeble all summer would ask, "Where you been preacher? I haven't seen you all summer." Keeble would explain he had been out holding meetings.

Marshall Keeble wrote a note to the *Gospel Advocate* in 1916 about A. M. Burton arranging for J. E. Acuff to teach the *G. Dallas Smith Bible Drill* lessons to the Jackson Street church.

Brother Burton furnished all the books. Keeble attended every one of those classes.

Fortunately Marshall Keeble started writing to the *Gospel Advocate* about his work. His white brethren requested him to do this. From this time, the movements of Marshall Keeble may be precisely traced. A good idea of Keeble's work is contained in his report for 1916. He preached 365 sermons, baptized 118, restored 47, visited 65 sick people, performed one marriage ceremony, preached four funerals, visited 36 places, and traveled 7,000 miles, and was paid $795.15. There were other gifts of clothing and provisions. His wife and children were sometimes with him. Minnie was a great help in teaching Bible classes and helping out with the singing.

During World War I Keeble was holding a meeting in Patton Junction, Alabama—a mining town—when his draft notice came. Keeble's wife neglected to send him the card. Learning about his draft notice upon returning home, he was afraid the draft board would send him right on into the army. Keeble hurried down town to the draft board to explain.

"Now what's your business?" demanded the draft board officer. Keeble presented his draft notice, "I got a call to enlist in the army." Upon examining the notice, he sternly reprimanded Keeble, "You are three weeks late. I ought to send you right now to the front. What's your story?"

Marshall Keeble could melt a heart of stone with gentle courtesy, "Cap, I was in a meeting at Patton Junction, Alabama. I wouldn't have disobeyed you for nothing."

The officer got a little sterner—"I've heard that one before too. You ought to be sent off right now to the front line."

Keeble came back, "No Sir, I was in a gospel meeting and I didn't know I was called. I wouldn't have disobeyed you." Keeble softened him up with his sincerity. He filled in the forms and in a few days the war was over. Keeble said, "I might near got in the army that day."

Keeble's first wife called him Marsh. When fame began to thrust itself on the young man, Minnie would caution him— "Marsh, you be careful what you say and do; and don't let anybody make you pack your suitcase back home!" Annie C. Tuggle told this story. No person has questioned the character of Marshall

Keeble who is now eighty-nine years old and who has lived an unstained life of unimpeachable integrity.

Marshall Keeble learned how to preach by listening to Campbell and Womack and he learned the art of "chart" and "blackboard" preaching from Joe McPherson. And he learned the art of religious discussion by debating with his father. Marshall Keeble's father finally came under the influence of a religious group in Nashville known as the "Do-Rights" who practiced "footwashing" and used water in the Lord's supper; and for twenty years Robert Keeble was the leading preacher among the "Do-Rights."

Keeble said it never occurred to him while growing up that he could dispute with his father. But after he was married and preaching the gospel, Keeble thought he could answer any man when it came to the Bible. When the proposition came up for religious debate between father and son, Keeble said, "You are a good father, but Poppa, I'd debate you as quick as I would anybody. Poppa, you are wrong." That debate got under way in the "Do-Right" building at the corner of Fourth Avenue and Highland in South Nashville. People came in large numbers to hear father and son debate. What Marshall Keeble called a "religious debate" would have baffled a parliamentarian and excited the envy of Alexander Campbell of Bethany College. If Keeble ever got bested in a religious debate, nobody who ever heard him thought so. His opponents to the man without a single exception quickly retired from the field, and not one ever claimed a victory, and not one returned to take him on a second time.

In 1916, Marshall Keeble was standing on the threshold of a unique fame unequalled in kind by any other evangelist in the whole passage of Restoration History. It was in this year he preached two nights in the home of a prosperous Negro farmer, Bose Crooms, who lived near Henderson, Tennessee. Bose Crooms, his wife, and two daughters were the only Negroes around Henderson who were members of the church of Christ.

Bose Crooms moved to Chester County from Union City, Tennessee. Keeble said he baptized Bose Crooms' eleven year old son in the swift waters of the Forked Deer River that was close by. Keeble said Bose Crooms loved that little boy who was his only son so dearly he followed Keeble and the boy out into the river for fear Keeble might let the child drown. The next year, October 11, 1917, Keeble preached a four night stand in a rented Methodist

37

meetinghouse in Henderson, Tennessee. Arrangements were made for Keeble to return to Henderson the following year.

The year 1918 marked the actual beginning of Marshall Keeble's fabulous career as a gospel preacher. In the issue of the *Gospel Advocate* dated February 11, 1918, Keeble wrote his *Confessions* in a few words. What follows is the keynote and the themes of the grand symphony of Marshall Keeble's life:

Things that we should be thankful for—

While sitting at home on account of such severe weather and studying God's Word, I can see so many things to be thankful for. I thank God for that dear old mother that brought me into this great world and instilled that great principle into me to love God, and for that father that labored hard to give to his family the necessities of life and took me by the hand and let me go to church every Lord's day. We need more parents like these; for a child reared this way will never depart from its training. At the age of fourteen I obeyed the gospel, and I am so thankful that I began to serve the Lord early in life, so I never learned so many evil habits that most young men learn. When about eighteen years old, I married a daughter of S. W. Womack. I never thought at first what a blessing it was to marry into this Christian man's family, but I am thankful now. If there ever was a Christian anywhere, this old servant is one. While I am young, I am trying to live humble and meek like him and I thank God for the impression his life has made on me. Some people send flowers and put them on the casket after death, but I believe in giving them while we live. I am a young preacher endeavoring to make a success in life; and if I can just make the man Brother Womack is, I will be so thankful. His success in life, in a material way, has not been very great, but I have reference to the great treasure he is laying up in heaven. He has established more churches and done more to keep digressivism out of this State than any colored man I know of anywhere; and had it not been for the instruction he received from such men as Brother David Lipscomb and Brother E. G. Sewell, he could not have succeeded as he has. I have been in conversation with him thousands of times on scriptural subjects, and he rarely ever finishes without mentioning one or the other of these great men. About nineteen years ago Brother A. C. Campbell decided to pull out from Digressivism, and he had courage enough to begin a mission in his own home. As soon as Brother Womack learned of it, he joined hand in hand with him, and they worked for some time this way, and the interest grew so we had to get a larger place to worship so we purchased a piece of property on the corner of Jackson Street and Fourteenth Avenue, North, known as the "Jackson Street Church of Christ," and we are so thankful for this work that these two worthy Christian preachers have done. Brother Campbell is nearly sixty years of age, but is yet active in the ministry, and I know of no man that is doing more to convert the world than he. As I have been closely connected with these two brethren for about twenty years or more, I can truthfully say they have suffered while preaching the gospel, and their wives need to be praised for their great endurance, and for all of this we thank the Lord. It was these two men that encouraged me to preach the gospel, and I shall never be through praising them and thanking God for such blessings. Neither of these men know that I am writing this article. I just thought it proper to say a few words about the good they are doing and have done. Brother Womack and Brother Campbell say that the *Gospel Advocate* has been second with them, and the Bible first.

Speaking concerning the *Advocate,* it has been a great help to me in studying the Bible. I have been reading it ever since I learned to read. My grandfather took it until his death; then, after I married into Brother Womack's family, I found it there. So I am still reading it, and may it go forth blessing the world as it did when that great and noble servant, David Lipscomb, lived. Some brethren think that the paper will not be what it used to be, but I believe such men as J. C. McQuiddy, A. B. Lipscomb, and T. B. Larimore are fully able in every sense to cause the paper to hold its present position in the world, and, like Joshua, they will lead us across Jordan. For all of these rich blessings we thank our Heavenly Father.

I want to thank the editors of the *Gospel Advocate* for publishing articles and reports from time to time.

Bose Crooms went to N. B. Hardeman about a meeting place in Henderson. Hardeman made arrangements for the Baptist meetinghouse. When the Baptist learned Keeble was coming to town, they went to N. B. Hardeman to renege on their agreement explaining "they were going to hold their annual conference." Keeble described the encounter, "So sorry, Mr. Brodie"; they said, "but they weren't sorry about nothing." Keeble always advised his white brethren to pay in advance when they rented a denominational meetinghouse for him to preach in. He said the Negroes were honest and would stick to their word. But once Keeble got to preaching the gospel, it was more than they could stand.

Hardeman arranged for Keeble to use the Oak Grove school located in a large Negro community about seven and one-half miles out of Henderson. N. B. Hardeman had served several years as superintendent of the Chester County schools. The meeting got under way on the third Lord's Day in July, 1918, and lasted three weeks. And what a meeting!

Eighty-four persons were baptized in the pond belonging to Plummer Bland, a white farmer who lived close by. Keeble went to the pond one day to baptize twelve. Standing in the back of a wagon, he preached to a large crowd and ended up baptizing thirty. Keeble said he noticed he was baptizing wet people. He asked, "Haven't I baptized you before?" He learned they were exchanging their dry clothing for the wet clothing of the newly baptized.

It never occurred to Marshall Keeble he was "proselyting" members of other churches when he came to a community. He came to preach the Bible and had too much sense to think religious division was right. Keeble had no "ecumenical" theories to preach—only the Bible. Anyhow, Keeble stirred up a "hornet's nest" around Jack's Creek, Tennessee, that has never been the same since. N. B. Hardeman was popular among the Chester County Negroes and they came to him with their complaints: "Mr. Brodie, that Keeble is a trouble-maker and he's

39

tearing up the churches." Hardeman explained Keeble could not be put out of a public building without showing cause. Hardeman advised them to get the leading Negro citizens to sign a complaint petition. All one day they went on foot and mule back canvassing the neighborhoods and returned with a petition filled with names.

As Hardeman ran down the list, he would say, Where is this or that prominent Negro's name, "Oh! Mr. Brodie, he's got him." Finally Hardeman responded, "It looks like he's just about got them all." Keeble said eyes were "popping" the last night of the meeting. There N. B. Hardeman was sitting on the stage with Keeble as big as life. Keeble said the Negroes were excited. "Just look there. He must be right. See Mr. Brodie sitting up there with him!"

And what a pair! N. B. Hardeman and Marshall Keeble! The likes of them will not be seen around Henderson anytime soon.

Marshall Keeble stayed in Bose Crooms' house during the Oak Grove meeting. Each night they rode several miles down the dusty road to the Oak Grove school house in a wagon with four or five seats filled with people. One night a wheel rim came off and went sailing by the mules. Keeble said he hopped off the wagon and chased that rim down just as it was passing ahead of the team. Word got back to Nashville, Tennessee, that Marshall Keeble was setting Chester County "on fire." They came down to see and went back to tell that the story was being fully and accurately told.

During the Chester County meeting, the Negroes were holding their annual Methodist conference in a Negro section near Henderson not far from Oak Grove. Keeble attended the meeting and spoke by invitation. He had all the Methodist preachers "stirred up," and they tried to debate Keeble which was like inviting a fish to a swimming match. The Methodist bishop knew the debate was unequal and ordered the disputants—"Just sit down! Sit down! I told you." Keeble said, "They obeyed that bishop—almost fell down." Whatever the reasons, the Methodist closed out their annual conference in Lucyville dating back to the time when Keeble first came to Henderson.

Keeble is described as "humble" by many who know and love him. But "humble" doesn't mean "servile." Keeble said he "never bowed to anybody but God," and no man ever lived who

40

showed a finer decency or more gentle courtesy to his fellow man. Keeble's company has been sought out by the great of his day. His kindness is as equally unfailing to the humblest of his race. May it be to the shame of any person who describes Marshall Keeble as an "Uncle Tom." Marshall Keeble has done what he could and no man can do more. Booker T. Washington lived the last of his days in the first of Keeble's life. Both men had an unashamed love for their race. Both did what they could with what they had to lift up the Negro race.

So in 1918 with justifiable pride Marshall Keeble reported for the *Gospel Advocate* four years of his work:

Year 1915—Sermons	240	Baptized	90	Restored	23	Miles traveled	5,260
" 1916— "	335	"	135	"	30	" "	5,000
" 1917— "	297	"	104	"	16	" "	6,497
" 1918— "	289	"	128	"	17	" "	6,295
Total 4 years	1,161		457		86		23,052

A meeting of a Billy Sunday or Gypsy Smith hardly created more excitement among white and Negro than a Keeble meeting. And there's another big difference. The work of Marshall Keeble over sixty years is standing and flourishing in this nation among thousands of both races who make up churches all over this land. No evangelist of any race among the churches of Christ can compare with this humble man of African extraction. And the Keeble "Oak Grove" meeting will live in history. This was the first church that Keeble started in a destitute field.

With the triumph of the Oak Grove meeting fresh in mind, Keeble moved then into Henderson, Tennessee. Nashville has often been described as the "Jerusalem" of the New Testament church. In a like manner, Henderson, Tennessee, the citadel of Freed-Hardeman College, is known wherever members of the church are preaching the gospel around the world. Keeble started another church in Henderson, Tennessee. He returned to Henderson a year later (1919) for another meeting with the church membership numbering more than a hundred. N. B. Hardeman attended the last service and brought words of encouragement. Keeble said he left his brethren cutting down trees to be carried to the saw mill for a new meetinghouse.

At the end of 1918, the "Happy Warrior" had been evangelizing four years. *Let it be said here that Marshall Keeble has been supported by his race.* There is no cause to show proof. There are thousands of Negro Christians now living baptized in Keeble meetings, and a similar number of white Christians who came out to enjoy Keeble and "the gospel back-fired on them." There are hundreds of churches and a host of gospel preachers who were inspired to preach as they watched this "diminutive man" handle and use the plain and simple New Testament "power of the gospel" as no other man has since apostolic times according to the thinking of many.

Keeble sent in a report to the *Gospel Advocate* in 1919: "I am glad I had the privilege of being present at David Lipscomb College on May 14, because I saw the need of Christian education as never before. Brother David Lipscomb put a coal of fire among the brethren before God took him, which will never die."

Marshall Keeble is sometimes described as being out of touch with the times. This is true. Marshall Keeble's age is now history and his life's work is legend. If the present younger generation who do not understand the bygone era of Keeble and would not fill vast auditoriums just to see and hear him at eighty-nine—their parents and grandparents of both races still do. They remember Keeble—not the victim of a period—but as one who shaped the character and destiny of New Testament Christianity as few gospel preachers have.

Keeble was reluctant in the early years of his ministry to go into the delta country of Mississippi. The "klan" activities there were more notorious in "talk" than action. Negroes had little to fear from the klan. But Keeble never hesitated to go into the hill country of Mississippi. He was preaching in Belen, Mississippi, around World War I. A great many Negroes loved him and came out in great numbers to hear him.

Their excitement was so great, the white people showed a lively interest by reprimanding their "farm hands." One planter said, "You just gone wild over this guy: you don't know where he's from. And now you've gone and left your church on the hill." Keeble said here he'd come out the next night—"A great big fellow with a wide-brimmed hat looking like he could eat you up." And Keeble added, "I'd say so many funny things about the Methodist and Baptists, he'd start laughing." That night he would go home carried away with Keeble's preaching.

The farmer would be up bright and early and out in the fields to tell his men, "I heard that man last night. He ought to been here a long time ago. Now every last one of you go out and hear him tonight." And one of his tenants had a reputation for being mean to his family. The planter would order him—"George, you hitch up the wagon tonight, and take your wife and children out to hear Keeble." And then following an afterthought, he added, "As a matter of fact, you round up everybody on the place and take them to hear that preacher." Keeble said, "He'd might near make them go, and here he would come riding up on his big saddle horse."

One one occasion, a white Baptist planter came down to the cabin where Keeble was staying to sit on the porch as was their custom—"Keeble, I thought I'd come down and talk awhile with you." Keeble said he was so friendly you would have thought he was a member of the church. It would be around noon and the farm hands would be standing around looking on. That night Keeble would baptize ten or fifteen of them. Keeble explained—"Many a white man got his dose along with the rest of them, and he just let up on his strictness on his farm hands."

Then some leading white citizen who heard about the "big stir" Keeble was causing would run into Keeble on Saturday—"How long you going to be here preacher?" And then he'd move on after a little more polite conversation. That night he'd come out and just be carried away with the sermon. Then he would start preaching—"I want all of you Negroes around here to come out and hear him. I want everybody in this town to hear that man." He would be too proud to come up and make his confession. But when the first white preacher came in, often he was the first one up to be baptized.

A white planter in Center Point, Arkansas, heard Keeble and asked him where he had come from. When Keeble told him Nashville, he responded, "You're the best Negro I ever seen from up north."—"Calling Nashville being up north!" Keeble added.

But Keeble was not welcomed everywhere he went. On the first Saturday in October, 1919, Keeble started a meeting in Colliersville, Tennessee, under a big tent. The attendance was good and the interest was running high. Many of them had never heard the pure gospel before. The Negroes were so enraged they reported to the white people that Keeble was trying to start a "race riot." A delegation came out and reported back in town "the preaching was good and just what they needed."

This is one occasion when the favorable sentiment of the white people did not help. Letters were left on the table threatening "personal injury to Keeble or to burn the tent" if he didn't leave the country at once. Finally they persuaded the man who owned the lot where the tent stood to order it moved. Keeble finished that meeting out fifteen miles down the road at Neshoba, Tennessee.

The manner in which the white Southerner addressed the Negro, Keeble said, was done in ignorance—"He thought that's what he ought to call me. He didn't mean a bit of harm." Many contemporary Caucasians are not as charitble in this respect as Keeble, and who feel that the mistreatment of the Negro in whatever form can only bring memories of shame.

Marshall Keeble stood on the threshold of the "Roaring Twenties" when fame with the "sound of a mighty rushing wind" was about to be thrust upon him. And Keeble would add to the confusion of the "Twenties" as he went everywhere preaching the gospel and "turning the world upside down!"

CHAPTER V

Turning The World Upside Down

Marshall Keeble's incomparable reputation as a great evangelist grew slowly in the 1920's. Religious meetings such as Keeble held in Oak Grove out from Henderson, Tennessee, were often repeated and just as spectacular. Keeble did not add a great deal of confusion to the "Roaring Twenties" until near their close. His preaching, however, created admiration wherever he went and was attended by numerous baptisms. Substantial members of the church such as N. B. Hardeman were solidly supporting him.

Keeble enjoyed a general recognition among the churches after his first famed meeting which he conducted in Tampa during 1927 which was followed by other sensational meetings in St. Petersburg, Lakeland, Bradenton, and Jacksonville, Florida. Coupled with the Florida meetings, he conducted the famed Atlanta and two Valdosta, Georgia, meetings in the opening thirties.

Marshall Keeble's relation to the Negro and the white races has often been discussed. No man has questioned his loyalty to his own race, nor his life long efforts to help elevate them spiritually and educationally. And no matter how Keeble's race may interpret or explain his relations to the white people, the fact goes undisputed that no other religious group in the South has singled out a lone Negro and heaped upon him more personal honors than on Marshall Keeble. Such honors that Keeble has received from both races would have pleased all and flattered most had they been similarly so honored.

Success followed Keeble wherever he preached the gospel. His reputation as a gospel preacher was solidly built in the 1920's. After the Florida meetings in the late twenties, white people started calling him all over the nation to preach to his race generally at the expense of the white churches. Individuals often offered to support Keeble if he would come and preach to the Negro community.

Keeble's life was not wholly given to preaching. He was devoted to his family. His only son Robert was never well. In hope of improving his son's health, he carried Robert in November of

1919 to Detroit, Michigan, thinking a change in environment would help the small boy. He got a job janitoring in the Maxwell Motor Company. He found on his arrival in Detroit, two small churches. One was a small mission group meeting on St. Antione Street in a store front. The other church was meeting on Ford Avenue in a schoolbuilding, and that congregation is still in existence. While he worked in Detroit, his wife mailed the *Gospel Advocate* to him each week. After spending the winter months in Detroit, Keeble made his plans to go South for his protracted meetings. His boss tried to hold him on the job, and wanted to know if he could make more money preaching: Keeble responded, "No sir, but my meetings start in May, and I've got to be there." He wrote in this connection for the *Gospel Advocate,* "I am now arranging for the 1920 protracted meeting season. My time for the first of July until November is engaged, and I will be glad to receive other calls from needy fields." Nothing unusual marked this preaching year; nor was this a year marked by one of Keeble's great meetings.

In 1920, Keeble chalked up one of his finest years though little fan fare attended his efforts. Many white people were dubious as to the value of preaching to the Negro race generally regarded by most as emotionally unstable and given to dark superstitions. Marshall Keeble thought little of this line of reasoning and said so.

One of the reasons for the unparalleled success of Marshall Keeble is to be found in the complete identification he makes with his own race. This has excited their admiration for him, and challenged white people to their shame to help push the Negro up. He reminded the white Christians when he wrote to the *Gospel Advocate* that when they were planning mission work abroad not to forget the Negro at their door:

To use all the time and money to reach foreign nations, and neglect your cooks, house girls, farm hands, chauffeurs, and nurses, I think is a serious and sad mistake: because if we can get the gospel to those who serve your homes and care for your little ones, you can put more trust in them and save them from ignorance of the blessed gospel of Jesus Christ.

Although the year of 1920 was not especially marked, lasting impressions were being deeply etched in Keeble's heart. His preaching work carried him into the deep South in places unlike Henderson and Nashville, Tennessee. In all the Southern states the Negroes were mostly ignorant, but their faith in the Bible was intense and sincere. There were the "white apologist" in the "deep South" who believed in the stability and character of the

46

Keeble   Keeble

Keeble   Marshall and Laura Keeble
                         just married

Negro race and were persistent that the gospel should be preached to them.

When the white people brought Keeble into Southern communities, it made the sectarians angry. "What are they doing bringing that man in here trying to mix the races?" Keeble said they didn't understand at first, but after a night or two they caught on.

Such a man who had confidence in the Negro was W. C. Graves in the West End church of Christ in Birmingham, Alabama. Every year when the budget for mission work was brought up, W. C. Graves without fail always raised the challenge—"What about the Negro living in our back yards?" The Birmingham church was finally goaded into action by his never failing annual remarks. Keeble came to this great Southern city the last of May in 1921 to preach the gospel to the Birmingham Negroes. What a "homecoming" it turned out to be!

During that meeting Keeble learned another way to get the white man to help him. In the first week of the Birmingham meeting, Keeble led the singing under the "big tent." And he could do that well when he had to. Interest grew every night until more people were outside the tent than under it. Finally the white brethren saw Keeble was being severely over-taxed with his double duties. W. C. Graves took over the chore assisted by Brother Mosely. During this meeting Keeble baptized a little band of "sanctified" people who were meeting in a hall. During that meeting forty-five in all were baptized. Keeble wrote to the *Advocate*—"If we had more white brethren like Brother Graves and those with whom he worships at West End, my race would be lifted out of darkness. These brethren did not give their money and stand back somewhere, but they came to every service and rendered every assistance possible, and the results were a great ingathering of souls for Christ."

One fact stands out in this Birmingham effort—Keeble had established a "bridge head" in the South. He learned he could trust his "white brethren." Almost half a century has passed since then. They stood with Keeble and have continued to stand where he stands and to sit where Keeble sits. White people generally came out to have a lot of fun listening to Negro preachers—not to learn anything. The arguments among the white Christians in Birmingham was that it would be a waste of money to bring the Negro the "naked gospel." They learned better after Keeble came. There

48

are some twenty-five Negro churches in Birmingham, Alabama, today.

Nineteen twenty-one was a good year for Keeble. He returned to Henderson, Tennessee, in July for the fifth straight year. In reporting his work to the *Advocate* he said, "I have been away from my family for about three months, and I have one more meeting to hold before I can be blessed with seeing them again."

This year was filled with "brand new" experiences. Every Keeble meeting was packed with excitement. Keeble was in Utica, Mississippi, in October. Lee Sweeney wrote A. M. Burton to send Keeble to Utica. Sweeney secured the meetinghouse of the "Sanctified Church." The second night the "sanctified" people sensed something was wrong and sent for their preacher in Jackson, Mississippi. He heard Keeble and knew "something was wrong" for the "Sanctified Church." But he never said a word. He returned the next Lord's day and suggested that Keeble be stopped and the doors shut. They obeyed him! The man boarding Keeble was so interested that the meeting should continue he went to the principal of the Utica Institute who turned over the school auditorium to Keeble. Each night Keeble preached to several hundred students and many others came including several disabled soldiers. When Keeble got home, A. M. Burton gave him an extra $12.50 in addition to his railroad fare.

Marshall Keeble returned to Henderson in November and preached a week. While there a white brother told Keeble about a Freed-Hardeman student who preached in the city jail and baptized four Negroes. Keeble reacted: "This shows the influence that this college has on these young men, and I pray that such men as Hardeman and Freed may live long on the earth."

Joe McPherson was not the only white preacher to hold a meeting in the Jackson Street church. Will Cullum conducted a meeting in the church in 1921. The Jackson Street church was suffering at that time because of a church division.

Keeble conducted fourteen meetings in 1921, baptized one hundred and forty, and restored fifty-nine. Eleven of the meetings were supported by the white people. Three missions were started. White churches in Birmingham and Albany, Alabama, and Martin, Tennessee, for the first time, put the Negro mission work in their annual budgets. Keeble conducted a meeting in Murray, Kentucky, that attracted people for miles around. They invited him to return for a thirty day meeting in 1922.

49

It could be said in a fashion, every Keeble year was better than the last and each one packed with more surprises than a "car load of cracker jacks." He returned to Birmingham in January of 1922, and preached a month in the "Sanctified People's" meetinghouse. Over half of them promised they would be baptized when he returned for a thirty-day meeting in May and they kept their word. A "Sanctified preacher" challenged Keeble for a debate on water baptism, foot washing, and operation of the Holy Spirit. Keeble said that the debate lasted four nights and "he had enough." The Negro church had grown to seventy-five with plans to build a meetinghouse.

Marshall Keeble somehow was around on the ground floor in every church activity almost from the day Alexander C. Campbell and S. W. Womack started the church in North Nashville. The first Hardeman-Pullias Tabernacle meeting in Nashville is now recorded in church history as the occasion when the church of Christ first came to the favorable attention of Nashville and the surrounding regions. Marshall Keeble attended the services and baptized two Negro girls who came forward during the meeting. Keeble said of that experience—"This meeting was a source of great strength to me, and I feel better prepared to tell the old story of the cross." In this or another of the Tabernacle meetings, N. B. Hardeman called on Keeble to come from the audience to the stage to say the closing prayer.

Sooner or later every great name preacher crossed the path of Marshall Keeble. Charley M. Pullias had encouraged Keeble in Birmingham and arranged for Keeble to hold a meeting in Murfreesboro, his birthplace.

Keeble preached in June of 1922 at the Jefferson Street church of Christ which was a split from the Jackson Street church. This was a firm step on Keeble's part to bring the factions together. Later in life Keeble began holding meetings at both churches around the beginning of each new year that for decades now has become a tradition.

No unusual circumstances marked Keeble's efforts in 1922. His work created high interest in some of the places. A second meeting in Martin, Tennessee, which Keeble conducted, attracted people for miles around. White people came to hear him who would not have listened to a preacher of the church of Christ of their own race under any circumstance. In July of 1922, Keeble

50

was back in Henderson for the seventh meeting with a packed house every night. A. G. Freed came out one night and spoke briefly to the gathering. In one of Keeble's meetings in Henderson, thirty-five white people were baptized by N. B. Hardeman.

From time to time A. M. Burton helped support Keeble's preaching as the needs arose. He paid his fare in 1922 to Washington, D. C., and twice to Sturgis, Mississippi. During this meeting Keeble refused to ride a saddled mule to the meeting grounds after a heavy rain and the roads were muddy. He chose to walk down the muddy road with the man and his wife in whose home he was staying. A. M. Burton generally gave Keeble a little over expenses. He wrote about his friend to the *Advocate*—"This good man will never know what a man he has made out of me. He picked me up and encouraged me when I was almost discouraged." Two of Keeble's 1923 meetings are outstanding. He singled out the meeting in the nation's capital because few people attended and no one was baptized. T. B. Larimore and his wife were present and that would take on a special meaning later in Keeble's life.

The meeting in Sturgis, Mississippi, that started September 16 is unique. It would be fair to say that no preacher in recorded history among the churches of Christ has preached in so many unusual situations from the shadow of the electric chair in the Tennessee State penitentiary to the "bush country" in Africa. In Sturgis, Keeble conducted his meeting in a grove of trees near a railroad. A large stack of cross ties were nearby. He asked the section boss to lend him the cross ties for pews—who responded with a "Yes, if you'll put them back like you got them." Keeble packed most of the cross ties until he got blisters on his shoulders.

Next he went to the nearby farm home and asked the white lady, "Would you mind me going down to find some old broken cotton plow lines and baling wire?" Permission was granted, but Keeble was admonished not to get good plow lines. Next he borrowed "pop" bottles from a nearby groceryman. Keeble filled them with coal oil and used the cotton plow lines for wicks. He strung them on baling wire which he fastened to the trees that circled the "cross tie" pews. Keeble said it was a pretty sight down in the valley at night—"looked like the place was lit up with electric lights." When the meeting was over the new converts told him—"Now Brother Keeble, we'll put these cross ties back." "They hadn't offered to put them there," Keeble said; and he stood back and enjoyed himself while those new Christians wore

51

blisters on their shoulders stacking those cross ties like he found them.

In 1923 Keeble conducted 18 meetings, baptized 208, restored 59, and started two new congregations. This was Keeble's best all round year. And he said—"I am glad to say that Alabama is in the lead in doing mission work among my race." What follows is typical of the relation that Marshall Keeble and A. M. Burton enjoyed till Brother Burton passed away:

> As an individual, Brother A. M. Burton is doing more to get the gospel to my race than any man I know of. He tells me that nothing does him more good than to hear of people obeying the pure gospel. I have just made a private report to him to help him enjoy Christmas. He has paid my railroad fare to Washington, D. C. and Sturgis, Mississippi twice this year, and now offers to pay my fare to California and return; and he always gives over what the fare comes to.

But every Keeble year was better than his last. On January 24, 1924, he entered the mission field in Oakland, California. This work was planned by T. B. Larimore. This was the first gospel meeting ever conducted in the San Francisco area by a Negro preacher of the church of Christ. Keeble didn't set the "golden hills" of California on fire. But it would be hard to find a place where Marshall Keeble preached any length of time that does not today boast of a thriving congregation.

Marshall Keeble cut a wide swath in 1924 that carried him from California to Alabama, the nation's capitol, and Wheeling, West Virginia. He turned again to Henderson, Tennessee, to preach in their new meetinghouse. Dorsey Hardeman, the son of N. B. Hardeman, gave the lot for the new meetinghouse. N. B. Hardeman came out one night to speak to an overflow congregation.

This general period marked the beginning of the Keeble's sensational debates that ran on into the thirties. He told how the debates came about:

> The Lone Oak church of Christ (white) in Paducah, Kentucky called me here to work among my people. I preached in a large well-lighted tent. While there I engaged in three debates. The first was with a sanctified preacher who endeavored to prove that baptism in water is not essential to salvation; the next, with another sanctified preacher who tried to prove that water instead of wine should be used in the Lord's supper; and the third with a "Do Right" preacher who tried to prove that foot washing was binding today. Each of these debates resulted in a victory for the truth, and the people rejoiced. Some who feared that these discussions would hurt the meeting were convinced that they were a help to the meeting.

Thirty-two were baptized and fifteen came from the "digressives."

The white brethren assisted Keeble in leading the song service. They engaged Keeble to return the following year for a thirty-day stand.

Marshall Keeble has always boosted the *Gospel Advocate* and the paper has never failed to boost his work. He wrote the paper—"After establishing a new congregation, the first thing I do is to get them to order the quarterlies published by the *Gospel Advocate.*"

This year was jammed from January to December with meetings. If anybody had doubted by now Keeble's direction, it was plain in this year that he was on his way up and out. The Lone Oak, Kentucky, meeting proved to be one of Keeble's greatest testing grounds as a religious debater the likes of which had not been seen before nor since. In all Keeble conducted twenty-one meetings in this year. He closed out 1924 in Henderson, Tennessee, helping them raise their last payment on their meetinghouse. Keeble wrote to the *Advocate*: "When I came into this country, the sects were real angry; but Brother N. B. Hardeman stood by me, and now many of those who were so opposed to the doctrine have been baptized and are harder fighters than I am."

The year 1925 was not especially marked by any sensations other than the year was filled with good work. However, the next year left Keeble with memories that he still talks about. A great friend of Keeble in the 1920's was Price Billingsley who set the stage for two of Keeble's most exciting preaching adventures.

In the twenties feelings were running high between the races. The average Negro was scared to death that he might say or do something wrong. For that reason Keeble did not deem it wise to go into the rich delta country of Mississippi. But as he looks back down the vista of the years, he says that Georgia and Arkansas were the states hardest in their treatment of the Negro. He preached once in an Arkansas community where a white planter shot a Negro Baptist preacher for interfering with his tenants. He visited Keeble's meeting and put a ten dollar bill in the collection plate.

Keeble started a meeting in February, 1926, in Summit, Georgia. The meeting caused a great commotion in the community. Keeble's most terrifying experience with the Ku Klux Klan happened during the meeting. The weather was cold, and the meeting was in a school house. As usual the white people came in large numbers to hear Keeble which did not please some. The klansmen said no white people were going to attend that meeting. It was a common fear that it was the practice of the klan "to drag" a man out of a house in the dead of night and "tar and feather" him or even worse. This was mostly just "talk."

About twenty-five klansmen one night suddenly stormed into the school house to everyone's surprise. After stomping up and down the aisles, they stormed out into the darkness leaving the door open. Keeble asked a Negro to shut it. He got up and sat down like he'd been shot. He saw the klansmen caucusing in the school yard. Keeble didn't know they were still outside. He backed to the door still preaching and slammed the door. Here they came rushing back in! The leader handed Keeble a note which he started silently reading. The leader ordered Keeble "to read it out"—"The Ku Klux Klan stands for white supremacy. Be governed accordingly."

Lesser men would have panicked. But not our man Keeble. He remembered the Bible admonition—"Agree with thy adversary quickly in the way least he turn and rend you." What white people don't fully understand about Keeble is his understanding of how white people think about the Negro. He has used his grasp of "white psychology" to great profit. On this occasion he said, "I have always known the white man is superior. They brought us from Africa and have lifted us up." Keeble with a rare flash of genius turned on the Negroes—"Now you treat these white folks right and they'll treat you right. They are your friends and they'll take care of you." Keeble baptized twenty-two in that meeting.

In the 1920's the Ku Klux Klan had the practice of going around to religious meetings laying money on the table to show their approval. Afterwards they would sit on the front benches with their "little eyes" peering through the white slits. On some occasions they came to frighten a man out of the country. Keeble preached all over the South when their activities ran to a feverish pitch. However, the fight was taken out of the klan when they learned so many of their members were also members of the church of Christ. They soon learned that the church members would draw a hard line between their loyalty to the church and the Ku Klux Klan, and that included "their preacher Keeble."

Keeble returned to Summit the following year. The leader who handed Keeble the note was a doctor and a Primitive Baptist. His Negro cook, whom Keeble baptized, recognized him. The doctor met Keeble on the street with a hearty welcome and told Keeble he was glad to see him back in town, and said if anybody bothered him, "Just let me know."

Keeble had an occasion for great rejoicing in May 26, 1926. When he preached for the Jackson Street church, he baptized three people including Keeble's "dear old mother." She had often said she was born a Methodist, lived a Methodist, and would die a Methodist.

On August 20, 1926, Keeble was in a meeting in Decatur, Alabama. While there his brethren arranged for him to preach in the Louisville and Nashville Railroad shops. Twice a week for three weeks Keeble for thirty minutes preached to the men in the shops. They would eat their dinner quickly as possible to listen to Keeble. The races were about half and half. When the whistle blew, Mr. Randolph, the boss, would let him preach a little longer. Keeble would lay his derby down somewhere and it would be half full of silver and dollar bills.

Keeble said he heard one of the crap shooters say—"Hell, I don't want to do right, but I want to give that fellow something." He turned to one of his companions and sternly ordered him, "Give that man something!"

Keeble told about holding a meeting in Florence, Alabama. There never was a better "street corner" preacher than Marshall Keeble. He went down to the town square. A Holiness preacher who had been in town all week was just finishing his sermon. He was accompanied by his wife who had a tambourine.

As the crowd started to break up, Keeble stepped forward— "Just a minute. I got a few things to say to you gentlemen this brother didn't tell you. I want to inform you that none of the apostles beat a drum and had their wives following them around with a tambourine. That's not in the Scriptures nowhere." Keeble is a crowd pleaser and they enjoyed him and all that he had to say that day.

When Keeble finished, the Holiness preacher and his wife were mad. Keeble described what happened: "I lit out down the alley and she grabbed me by the collar. Her husband was running along to see if I would hit her. I didn't intend to do nothing. He was going to knock me down. He was running along beside us to protect her. She had a good hold on me, but I was carrying her so fast, she turned me loose."

The next Saturday, the "Holiness preacher" and his wife were back, but nobody would listen to them. The people got the word around—"That Keeble is a real Christian." Some said—"If I'd been Keeble I would have knocked him down."

In 1926 Keeble visited six states, preached 363 sermons, conducted 21 meetings, baptized 163, and 31 were restored. His annual meeting at the Jackson Street church was now a tradition. A. M. Burton arranged for him to broadcast the January 9, 1927, services at Jackson Street over the radio station WLAC and again in March.

Keeble's famed five weeks Tampa meeting was held April 17, 1927. He preached in the digressive's meetinghouse for two nights until the tent came. Interest grew from the beginning. At first there was plenty of room for the white people under the tent since about fifteen Negroes came the first night. Finally the white people had to move out. Four Baptist preachers attacked what Keeble taught "because they didn't know any better." He gave them thirty minutes a piece each night to show Keeble was wrong.

T. A. Northcutt described in the *Advocate* what happened in meetings such as the one in Tampa: "The minute he moves to a new town, they will begin to fight back, and you know what that will do. Only one opponent so far, and he is too slow to catch a cold, but keeps fighting back, and Brother Keeble just knocks him unconscious every time, and he cannot even find it out."

Ninety-nine people were baptized including four preachers. Each night they had to go about five miles to the Hillsboro River to baptize. About a dozen white people offered their cars. One man hauled them in his new Packard. He would have them get in wet as they could be. Keeble said there was a time "he wouldn't have hauled a Negro dry." His car was a month getting dry from hauling so many wet Keeble converts.

Keeble said on one evening when he was baptizing a lady in the Hillsboro River, a big alligator came floating by and the woman was terrified. Keeble assured her: "Oh, he's all right!" And baptized her without further incident.

Nineteen hundred and twenty-seven turned out to be Keeble's greatest year so far. Now he stood a solid champion. Nobody disputed the fact. His first Tampa, Florida meeting started a "chain reaction" of Keeble meetings all over Florida.

S. F. Morrow managed the Tampa meeting and was a great

Keeble baptizing, Fort Smith, Arkansas

Keeble baptizing,
St. Petersburg, Florida

Keeble baptizing, Tampa, Florida

help to Keeble. He stood around watching the Negroes come to the meeting. Those that came the second time were approached by Brother Morrow.

S. F. Morrow was one of Marshall Keeble's true friends. The name of S. F. Morrow is destined to live through two of his grandsons—M. Norvel Young, President of Pepperdine College, and James O. Baird, President of Oklahoma Central College. He grew up around Clarksville, Tennessee, after the War between the States. He worked hard to support his wife and family. He promised his wife when they could sell their property for $50,000, they would move to Nashville to educate their children in the Nashville Bible School.

Norvel Young said his mother, Ruby, was thirteen when they moved to Nashville. She told how her father got people to go to Bible study on Sunday morning. Many were sharecroppers who didn't have shoes for their children. S. F. Morrow had his children to go bare-footed to church which caused some embarrassment to Young's mother, Ruby. Later he carried this interest in evangelizing the poor in tent meetings. He would rent a tent, pay the transportation cost, and send young preachers from the college to preach. S. F. Morrow was always interested in personal work and never overlooked the opportunity to talk the Bible with white or black, high or low.

Marshall Keeble remembers and appreciates the help S. F. Morrow gave him in those early times. Keeble described how Brother Morrow went about his work in Tampa. "It helped a colored man to see a white man interested in him." Brother Morrow would approach a Negro—"I saw you here last night. How do you like the preaching?" He would get his address and visit him the next day, and Keeble would baptize him that night. Brother Morrow told Keeble—"You're doing the greatest work I ever saw."

The Gary church of Christ sponsored the meeting. It was the smallest and weakest church in Tampa and generally regarded as a mission point. When the meeting got "red hot and roaring" most every white Christian in Tampa came. Keeble especially remembers Price Billingsly who first encouraged that meeting and gave $100 for its support.

Keeble conducted another of his sensational meetings this year in August just two blocks from Lane College (Methodist) in Jackson, Tennessee. Bishop Isaac Lane attended several nights. One Lane professor accused Keeble of preaching false doctrine and later wished he hadn't. He wanted to know if Keeble knew the Greek on Acts 2: 38. Keeble said—"The way I talk English you see I can't speak it very well." Keeble said he had the Greek New Testament "shelled" by the finest Greek scholars in the world into English. He called for a show of hands in the audience for all who could read Greek. "Not a hand went up." Keeble then sternly reprimanded the Lane scholar for bringing up the subject in the first place. Keeble won again when he extended the invitation and seven came forward. Any preacher who challenged Keeble for a debate before one of his vast audiences wished he hadn't later. Keeble said some preacher from Lane University would jump him, and "he had to shoot one every night."

Keeble baptized fifty-eight in that meeting and the white people provided a nice meeting place for the new disciples to worship. In September Keeble was in Sheffield, Alabama, for a meeting. N. B. Hardeman and B. C. Goodpasture made it a point to come by for a visit with him. Keeble enjoyed those visits. They were his "advisers" and helped Keeble through many a problem.

Keeble had a full year in 1928. He conducted a three weeks meeting in Florence, Alabama, beginning June 17 with this comment—"Many white people came thinking that we conducted our meetings like my race generally does with a great deal of excitement, but they were disappointed. Many of the best white people in town came every night." He wrote a letter to A. M. Burton published in the *Advocate* dated October 17, 1928: "As you are greatly interested in my mission work, I am glad to inform you that I have broken all of my former records this year in the way of visible results. To date I have baptized 343. . . . Last year the number baptized was 295. I am sure this news makes you happy."

Marshall Keeble remembers 1929, and not because of privations brought on by poverty of the times. Keeble was standing on the threshold of an unparalleled fame enjoyed by few other preacher in modern times. The first part of 1929 was a continuation of the 1927 Tampa, Florida, success story.

The work in Lakeland, Florida, began February 5, 1929, where a church of sixty-five was started. The next church Keeble started was in St. Petersburg. In this meeting ninety-two were baptized. J. Roy Vaughan was preaching for the white church in St. Petersburg and gave his hand to teach the young struggling group of Negro disciples one night a week. P. G. Millen wrote to the *Advocate* that three months of work in Florida were planned for Keeble. He stayed fourteen weeks, baptizing 202 people in the meanwhile. In Lakeland, Florida, one white brother led singing every night, until Keeble said, "We baptized a good songleader and turned the song service over to him." Keeble's white brethren stood mightly by him furnishing their cars to carry the people to the baptizing place or whatever else needed to be done. Keeble recommended Luke Miller to come to St. Petersburg, April 14, 1929. Miller divided his time between Lakeland, Tampa, and St. Petersburg.

Keeble followed the budding flowers back to Tennessee. In May Keeble was preaching in a meeting in Bell Buckle, Tennessee. He started a meeting the last of May in Montgomery, Alabama. They told Keeble that was the hardest place in the South to get his people to listen to the gospel. The prospects were not encouraging at the first. Before the meeting ended, more people stood outside the tent than were packed under it. That included a large number of white people.

Keeble preached in another meeting in Birmingham. Late August found him in Fort Smith, Arkansas. That meeting resulted in eighty-one baptisms. Keeble wrote for the *Advocate*: "A. M. Burton agreed to pay my railroad fare to Fort Smith, but when his check came, it was twice the amount of my fare."

Keeble was again in Henderson for a meeting in October and he said—"Brother Hardeman invited me to come to chapel to hear Brother S. H. Hall make an address, and after Brother Hall had finished, he asked me to make a talk, and they said I did well. Brother Hardeman for fifteen years has done much to help me in my evangelistic work. He has recommended me to come to the strongest churches we have today." This is a good place to say that N. B. Hardeman and A. M. Burton were in Keeble's corner from the start. Both were unparalleled church leaders in this century. It is not surprising they found a genuine article when they discovered spiritual dynamite in the "five foot four Keeble" who stands now taller than mountains.

Keeble remembers one meeting he conducted in Houston, Texas, for most of November supported by the white people. The song services were led by a physician, Dr. Glover Speer, who, Keeble said "was a great lover of the church." He enjoyed the meeting so much he gave Keeble a personal check for $50.00.

What Marshall Keeble, however, remembers was a trip to see the Gulf of Mexico. Dr. Speer arranged for a small private dining room. When the waitress came with the menu, the physician assured her what she saw was in good order since previous arrangements had been made. Keeble closed his year out in the deep South around Florence, Alabama. A great preacher was in the land. And the prominent leaders of the church knew it. So the story of Marshall Keeble has never stopped. It just grows.

CHAPTER VI

Never Man Spake

Marshall Keeble's reputation as a great evangelist was neither won over a brief spell nor at little cost. He won the hearts of people and their respect wherever he traveled with his never failing humility, and by preaching the gospel as they had never before heard it proclaimed. His efforts were crowned with success that began with his first talk in the Jackson Street Church.

Two early meetings of Keeble stand out—the Oak Grove meeting, out from Henderson, Tennessee, and the first Tampa, Florida, efforts. Keeble's growing fame became such that never after the 1930's would there be enough time to accept all the preaching invitations. Keeble returned to Florida in March, 1930, for another meeting in Tampa. P. G. Millen, one of Keeble's loyal white friends, had moved in the meantime to Jacksonville, Florida. Arrangements were then underway for Keeble to come to Jacksonville.

Keeble's next memorable Florida meeting was in St. Petersburg. The work in St. Petersburg resulted from the concern of two white men—"Pop" Richardson and his son-in-law, M. A. Dye, for a Negro, Lonnie Smith, who worked as a general handyman for them in their grocery store. A tent was pitched through the efforts of Dye and Richardson in a Negro community and Keeble preached several days with little results. The tent was moved to a new location a short distance away, and Keeble baptized ninety-six. Dye and Richardson furnished two of their houses—one for a meetinghouse and home for the preacher.

Keeble was busy during 1930 preaching a total 396 sermons—averaging more than a sermon a day. He preached almost continuously for forty-six weeks. He conducted a total of fifteen meetings baptizing 420 persons. Nineteen of that number were preachers. Twenty-nine were won from the "Digressives," and six new congregations were established.

Keeble conducted a June meeting in Valdosta, Georgia, in 1930. The white church there arranged for the meeting and supported it with their money and presence. A. B. Lipscomb, the Valdosta preacher, had to be away at the time.

Keeble tent meeting

Keeble at the blackboard

Marshall Keeble and William Lee

In Valdosta, Keeble would be challenged by some sectarian preacher every night. One preacher arose after Keeble invited him to the platform. Several of his members had been baptized by Keeble, and he was greatly agitated. He said, "The reason this man baptized you is because you never got religion in the first place." That was tailormade for Keeble who instantly agreed with him—"He's right. You never 'got religion.'" Then he would quote James 1: 27—"Religion is something you do—not something you get."

One Lord's day Keeble baptized fifty-nine in a heavy rain storm. On the following Sunday, Luke Miller baptized sixty-nine before coming out of the water. Eleven came from the "digressive." A total of one hundred and sixty-three were baptized. White people came from miles around to the Valdosta meeting. The Negroes got under the tent the best they could and the overflow spilled over the tent grounds. They said, "A great prophet has come among us."

Another meeting deserves special attention that Keeble conducted in December, 1930, at Ripley, Mississippi. Sheriff William Burton McBride, who was an elder of the church, invited Keeble to come down to eat all of his meals in the jail with the prisoners. Keeble learned that McBride never wore a weapon in discharging his duties as sheriff.

Keeble returned to Valdosta, George in 1931, for a repeat performance. All things were prepared for Keeble, and what a surprise it turned out to be! This meeting too was one of the most memorable in Keeble's life. B. C. Goodpasture sat nightly on the stage with Keeble. B. C. Goodpasture engaged a "court reporter" in Valdosta to take down Keeble's sermons in shorthand. Keeble was first annoyed, but got used to her presence. Her writing hand became swollen because Keeble spoke an unbroken stream of words unlike courtroom conversation. A doctor advised her that she was suffering a simple "muscle fatigue" and had no cause to worry. That book of sermons with a short biography was published under the title *Biography and Sermons of Marshall Keeble*. More copies of this work, according to Goodpasture, have been sold than any other single item published by the Gospel Advocate Company.

Following the publication of the book of sermons, Foy E. Wallace, Jr., at that time minister of the church of Christ in Seminole, Oklahoma, wrote B. C. Goodpasture:

Brother Goodpasture, you have done a great work for the church in compiling Brother Keeble's sermons in book form. The books came yesterday, and I took one and began reading it, and so did my wife and her mother. It was so interesting that we read it through without putting it down. When the telephone rang, I kept my book in hand and continued, when I had hung up the phone receiver, until I had finished it. The plain, simple message of the gospel with his simple illustrations make it easily one of the best books for untaught people in the Bible that I have ever read.

Keeble always boarded with a leading Negro family when he came to "plow in new grounds." At times it went something like this—"You are going to stay with old Aunt Mary. She was my nurse when I was baby." In a few days Keeble would baptize her. Since the church was not established—none were members of the church.

In Valdosta, Georgia, Keeble, Luke Miller, and his wife stayed with a Baptist lady and her husband. Keeble said—"If we'd been easily offended, we would have left there. One night the Baptist lady obeyed the gospel. "Her husband was a hot man," Keeble said, "but I acted like I didn't know he was mad as he could be." Luke Miller's wife left on her way to the meeting tent with a basket holding the baptismal garments. Keeble said after she was baptized "that house was on fire—that man was mad enough to fight when we got back from services that night."

On August 10, 1931, Keeble started his famed Atlanta, Georgia, meeting. There was not a single Negro member of the church in Atlanta when he began. The meeting was sponsored by the West End congregation. H. Clyde Hale was minister of the church at that time. The meeting had been booked in advance. The West End elders wrote Keeble the "depression" had stripped them of money. Keeble wrote—"I'm coming anyway."

Hale carried Keeble on his arrival out to the tent located on Ashby Street right in the heart of a fine Negro neighborhood. Hale was pleased—"How do you like it?"

Keeble said—"You got the tent in the wrong place." And he added "I might as well shot Hale. He was in the air till I said that." Keeble told Hale the people in the neighborhood won't come under the tent. "Where do the common people in Atlanta live?" Clyde Hale offered to ride Keeble through Atlanta. First, Keeble wanted to see the elders. The first elder ran large wholesale grocery establishment who was peeved with Keeble. Keeble told him—"Now if you just have a check for me, I'll take it. I didn't come for money, I came to save souls." Keeble added—"If I wanted to know how to run a wholesale grocery store, I'd come to you. But I just know my preaching."

The elder told Hale, "Carry him to the other elders—If they agree it's all right with me." The others agreed like Keeble knew they would.

He found his location on Simpson Street among the hard working class. He rented it from a Jew for $50.00, and he wouldn't take a cent after he heard Keeble, and told Keeble—"You can't take it away. It'll be there when you get through." The church Keeble started stands there today.

The preceding day a cloud burst had turned the lot into a sea of mud. Keeble helped to erect the tent, and so did Clyde Hale, dressed in a white linen suit. Approximately twenty colored and twenty white people came the first night. The tent was half full the second night. From that night on the tent overflowed. There was not a single response to the meeting the first week.

Keeble said about forty rough looking men with overalls on and no respect showed up when the meeting started. They were pretty harsh in Atlanta about that time. Negroes homes had been dynamited and the blame fastened on the Ku Klux Klan. When they came to Keeble's meeting they were dressed up for anything that might happen. They came to have a real "hoe down." "The preaching was so good," Keeble said, "those fellows came back the next night all dressed up with their collars buttoned and their neck ties on. You wouldn't have known them, and they came back every night."

About the second week of the meeting, a "Holiness" preacher, Bishop Swanson, came driving up in a Cadillac. He marched up to the platform when Keeble invited anybody who had something to say about the gospel he was preaching. Swanson was carrying a "sword cane." When Bishop Swanson came up, Luke Miller politely "arrested" the cane with the concealed sword. Luke said he was afraid Keeble would make him "so mad" he might use it But Keeble said, "He didn't mean no harm." But he was a "hot man" and he told Keeble, "There was a good feeling in this town before you came." Anyhow Keeble ended the whole affair by baptizing the "bishop" afterwards.

People poured in vast numbers into the tent ground the third and fourth weeks of the meeting. Because of the passing street cars disturbing the meeting the polite Georgia Power Company or-

66

dered their motormen to cut off the power on the streetcars as they coasted off the hill by the meeting grounds. Anonymous calls came to M. A. Hornsby, Chief of Atlanta Police, to kill Keeble and whip Clyde Hale. Keeble didn't learn this until the meeting was over. One hundred and sixty-six were baptized in that meeting. And that one meeting inspired a missionary spirit in Atlanta as nothing before had.

Luke Miller led the singing. Keeble stated they started that meeting with Luke Miller, Keeble, and Luke's wife singing hymns, and a few Negroes ambled over to join the few white people who came. Keeble said he and the Millers could "sing like mocking birds." That's how they "decoyed" the neighborhood under the tent. Keeble then preached. "My, how he could preach!" S. H. Hall described his feelings after the meeting—"I had to stand, but I could stand flatfooted and listen to Keeble preach three hours and never grow tired. . . . The doctrines and commandments of men and human organizations fall before him as shrubbery before an army tank."

Among those making the confession was a young man who had studied for the Catholic priesthood. He made his confession with the Negroes under Keeble. H. Clyde Hale exclaimed—"It was the most wonderful meeting I have ever witnessed. As many as 2500 people came to hear Keeble and never was there less than one thousand people." The West End church paid Keeble $250.00 for the meeting.

Keeble enjoys telling about the meeting he conducted in late summer in Muskogee, Oklahoma, where J. W. Brents preached. Keeble came late for the meeting and J. W. Brents was hot under the collar. A great deal of advertising had been done and all things were ready. Keeble said Brents was red-faced and mad when he met Keeble at the train and told him—"Keeble, you lied to me! Keeble said he was so busy telling him that I'd lied that he could not say—"hiddy" to me.

Keeble countered Brother Brents, "I said I'd be here on that date if the Lord willed it."

Brents said—"It's not in the letter; you didn't say it!" Keeble made J. W. Brents take that one back. Keeble always put that in a letter and hadn't failed this time. Keeble set all Muskogee in an uproar while he was there.

A. M. Burton wrote a special letter to the *Gospel Advocate* requesting they print a letter from J. W. Brents to Burton about the meeting:

Muskogee, Oklahoma, 910 East Broadway, October 8, 1931.—Dear Brother Burton: Brother Keeble, knowing your interest in his work and how much you rejoice over his success, suggested that I write you about his greatest meeting, which he has just closed here. For three weeks he battled as hard as any man I have ever seen in the pulpit. He is as calm in the very midst of every kind of cross fire by his enemies as you or I would be at our desks. Nothing ever seems to confuse him; and if ever a man had enough to provoke him to anger and irritation, he certainly had it here. One of the preachers took an hour of his time one night trying to show that Keeble was wrong. He replied to all he had to say in about fifteen minutes and gave an exhortation and invitation and some twenty made the confession. He seems as wise as a serpent and as harmless as a dove.

Hundreds of white people came to hear him that never would have heard a white preacher. Many of these are convinced. We have already baptized several, and will baptize many more, as a result of his splendid work. There were two hundred and four baptized of his own race. We have baptized a Cherokee Indian as a result of his work also.

When the time came for Keeble to go to St. Louis for a scheduled meeting, Brents said, "You can't go."

Keeble said, "I got to go. If I stay I'll have to tell another lie."

Brother Brents was willing, "Tell another one." Brother Keeble said and Brother Brents had many a good time over those "two lies" that Keeble told, and the last one at Brother Brents' instigation.

In November of 1931 Keeble conducted the sensational Bradenton, Florida, meeting and baptized 296 of his own race in the Manatee River. By October of 1932, the number baptized increased to 450 and in two years time grew to 700. John R. Vaughner of St. Petersburg, Florida, came to preach for them. They built a new meetinghouse that would set 800 people, and a home for the preacher. At that time, it was the largest Negro church in America. The Bradenton work was due to the interest of D. B. Whittle who furnished most of the financial assistance.

Keeble finally held the gospel meeting in Jacksonville, Florida. The Ku Klux Klan was active at that time. The meeting started and large numbers of white people attended the meeting. The klansmen came one night and ordered all the white people outside the tent. The meeting continued without further incident. The klansmen sat on the front porches of the Negroes who were of their same religious persuasion to keep, not so much the meeting under surveillance, but the white people who attended. Marshall Keeble is now an old man. All of this is ancient history. What no one seemed to know at that time how utterly defeated they were the moment they began to attack this humble Negro who never lost a skirmish much less a battle with either black or white when he stood to preach the gospel.

P. G. Millen, who had recently come from Tampa, was a loyal friend to the Negro converts. One night several klansmen came into the hall where Millen was teaching the Bible to the Negro Christians ordering him to stop meeting with the Negroes with the usual threat of "tar and feathering" or something worse. P. G. Millen told them—"I am not going to promise you anything. But I'll tell you this, when you come back you had better bring your tar and feathers." That ended the matter.

Just to catalogue Keeble's meetings would be a formidable task. Keeble's efforts in 1932 was a continuous repetition of his earlier work. After Keeble's great Florida and Georgia meetings, the years ahead would be filled with unpredictable meetings under all kinds of circumstances.

The year of 1932 was one of sorrow for Marshall Keeble. Minnie Keeble passed away December 11, 1932, at the age of fifty-three. Her funeral service was conducted in the Keeble home on Jefferson Street in the presence of a large crowd of friends and loved ones. The funeral was preached by S. H. Hall and O. L. Aker of Florence, Alabama. Marshall Keeble was in a meeting in the Middle West when he learned of her serious condition. He stayed by her bedside the last two weeks of her life. She was buried in Greenwood Cemetery in Nashville.

Keeble's preaching intinerary took on a pattern in the early thirties. Keeble said when cold weather came "he would duck back to Florida with the alligators." That was just changing homes for him. Occasionally he would work a California trip in or a Texas tour. When spring time came in Tennessee, Keeble headed North. Keeble was a "seasonal preacher" preaching in season and out of season at all times.

Keeble said when he first went to Florida, he would go all the way to Bradenton or Miami without a place to stop. That changed in the 1940's. Keeble said it would take about a month to go to either place stopping at all the churches he had established along the way. Keeble enjoyed those Florida trips, but he didn't go down for a vacation. He preached somewhere every night. When Keeble became president of the Nashville Christian Institute,

Luke Miller and John Vaughner feared that would end his Florida meetings. That never happened! "I never let nothing stop me from preaching the gospel, and establishing new congregations all over the country," Keeble explained in this connection.

In September 1933, Marshall Keeble conducted a meeting in Clinton, Oklahoma, and Lonnie Smith of St. Petersburg, led the singing. Thirty-five responded including a Methodist and a Baptist preacher. Keeble preached three times over the radio from Elk City through the courtesy of C. E. McGaughey. Crowds ranging from 500 to 3000 attended the night meetings. During the first week, Keeble was asked to speak at the day meetings of the Methodist Church. Every sermon was directed at the roots of Methodism. Finally the Methodist preacher said, "Brother Keeble, I am convinced; now preach to my people!" The preacher was baptized!

Marshall Keeble found his second wife through the help of his friend Percy Ricks. Laura Catherine Johnson, Keeble's second wife, was born August 6, 1898, in Corinth, Mississippi, to Luke and Susan Johnson. There were seven girls and three boys in the family. Percy Rick's wife, known to the Johnson family as "Bill," practically reared her brothers and sisters. The father worked in an iron foundry and the mother was a nurse. Laura Johnson Keeble finished No. 2 High School in Corinth, Mississippi.

When Keeble began to think seriously of marrying, he told Percy Ricks—"Some of you boys ought to find me a good wife. I can't live single the rest of my life young as I am." Percy Ricks, Keeble's brother-in-law, helped pick out Laura for Keeble and urged Keeble to begin courting her—"You get her, and you are going to get the best girl in the Johnson family." Ricks cautioned Keeble—"I don't say this because she's my sister-in-law, but because I think she deserves a good man."

This was tailor-made for Keeble—"What about me deserving a good woman?" Keeble would catch Ricks in a crowd later and tell the story—"Ricks told me I'd get the best rose in the Johnson flower garden, and I think I did." Keeble said Ricks sometimes got a little peeved when he teased a little too hard.

Keeble said—"It always disgusted me to see a preacher flirting around with a woman. So I just decided I'd correspond with her. I was never in my wife's company five minutes alone. I would see her in meetings."

M. Keeble and S. L. Cassius   R. N. Hogan and M. Keeble

John Vaughner and M. Keeble   Luke Miller

Marshall Keeble started off his courtship by writing her a letter. Percy Ricks had told Laura what she should do if such a letter came. Laura was living and taking care of her aged mother. She was somewhat afraid of the prospect of marrying Keeble. He was a preacher and twenty years difference in their ages gave her cause for concern. And Laura added—"I was afraid I couldn't come up to being a preacher's wife." Laura was in no hurry to marry Keeble with the explanation—"I didn't want to be too quick to answer or to say anything I couldn't come up to."

Keeble waited a long time between letters from Laura; and about time he started reading one, the letter closed. Keeble remarked—"She never did much talking—even now she doesn't talk much. But I was talkative and I thought you didn't love me if you weren't talking." Finally Keeble went down to Corinth to ask for Laura and the wedding date was set.

Keeble bought a new Chevrolet with wheels mounted on the front fenders and headed for Mississippi with Luke Miller driving. Keeble was running late for his wedding. Luke would speed up. Keeble would tell him to slow down. At the Jim Reed Chevrolet Company, the salesman advised Keeble not to drive the car more than thirty miles per hour. Luke would say—"We are going to be late for the wedding!"

Keeble would respond—"I don't want this car ruined. The time's already past. You'll have the car ruined, and you'll have it ruined before the wedding."

When Keeble had previously approached B. C. Goodpasture about performing the ceremony, Goodpasture told him—"I'll marry you anywhere east of the Mississippi and south of the Ohio." Goodpasture said he didn't want to travel so far; and Keeble responded—"You can marry me in lots less territory than that."

B. C. Goodpasture on the date of Keeble's wedding, April 3, 1934, was in a meeting in Florence, Alabama. He drove over to Corinth; Keeble wasn't there. He came driving up more than an hour late. Goodpasture told him—"She's backed out!"

Keeble knew better—"No, sir, she hasn't backed out." Brother Goodpasture asked Keeble if he wanted a long or short ceremony. Keeble said—"Doesn't matter—whatever you think is appropriate." Keeble almost broke up his own wedding with his "amens." The ceremony was performed in the home of Laura

Keeble's mother. Their friends wanted to know where the Keeble's were going on their honeymoon. And they learned—"he's going to take her right back with him to Nashville."

If Marshall Keeble has any faults, you can't pry them out of his friends or detractors—if there are such. Laura says Marshall Keeble has his failings. He likes to talk, and he wants me to be quiet and sit down and listen to him. She said he has always had his way of doing things. "So I have to let him go to his extent and then I take over." Not until recent years would he allow Laura help pack his suitcase. For a third of a century Marshall and Laura Keeble have lived together. Keeble had a good first wife and is equally blessed with a second wife.

It was Keeble's practice to hold a meeting for his own people generally supported by white people who attended in large numbers and often out numbered the Negroes ten to one. He held a meeting in April of 193, in Houston, Texas, supported by the Heights Church. Burton Coffman was minister at that time. Two tents were stretched side by side and filled to capacity every night with both races. In July he held two meetings simultaneously— he preached in Little Rock nightly and held day services in Conway, Arkansas.

One of Keeble's interesting revivals was conducted in May of 1934, in Chattanooga, Tennessee, in a large circus tent seating 1500 people. Thirty-two persons were baptized including six white persons.

The meeting ran for thirty days. Keeble still talks about the "Keeble train" that was hooked on behind the Miami bound Dixie Flyer bringing his Christian friends from Nashville to Chattanooga. The cars were side tracked at Union Station. The "circus tent" was pitched at Five Points across from Union Station. Percy Ricks, who is still a fireman on the Southern Railroad, made the arrangements for the "Keeble train" that came down on a Sunday of the meeting. The trip was advertised in the Nashville newspapers as the "Keeble train."

In the Chattanooga meeting, a "holiness" Negro woman started "to dance and shout down" Keeble's meeting. Two white men "red faced" with anger started to hustle her away. Keeble said her husband, about as "red faced" as the white men and ready to protect her, got up by her side. Keeble knew the meeting would be ruined if they so much as touched her. He commanded his

73

white friends—"Leave her alone, brethren, let that lady alone." Keeble just waited until she had shouted and danced herself to exhaustion then she meekly took her seat. Keeble said—"We won a great victory for the Lord that night."

Keeble headed for California in November of 1934 to run meetings through the following February. He conducted meetings in Los Angeles, Santa Anna, Bakersfield, Fresno, Riverside, and San Bernadino. It was during this trip that Keeble met William Lee. What a team they made—Keeble preaching and William Lee singing! Their names were almost synonymous through a part of the late thirties and early forties. Hugh Tiner gave Keeble one whole hour of his radio program "Take Time To Be Holy" over KGER, and a part of other programs. Keeble concluded that tour in a meeting in Phoenix, Arizona, on his way back home.

Keeble preached in Lawton, Oklahoma, a meeting that closed August 17, 1934. The number attending grew from 1200 to 5000. The whole city was aroused. A Baptist moderator from Reno challenged Keeble for a debate. "The second night the Baptist preacher took sick and had to be carried home. The truth was more than he could stand." Keeble described those preachers: "The poor things would challenge him for a debate because they didn't know any better." Many a person came out just "to enjoy Keeble" and left determined to live the rest of his days as a Christian.

In September of 1935 Keeble baptized a Negro lawyer and three preachers in Tyler, Texas. People came from miles around to hear Keeble preach. The complaint is sometimes made that Keeble has not baptized prestige people in his race. But that is debatable. There is no question that a legion of "quality" folk among the white race were baptized as a result of Keeble's preaching. Sooner or later most every leading member of the church came into Keeble's life. When he was in Mexia, Texas, during 1935, G. P. H. Showalter, editor of the *Firm Foundation* came up to engage him for a meeting in Austin, Texas.

The number of people Marshall Keeble has baptized grows yearly. When Keeble came to Tampa, Florida for his first meeting, not a single Negro congregation existed in the whole state. Eight years later there were twenty church of Christ congregations and 8000 members in Florida. While Marshall Keeble never kept an accurate record of the number of people he baptized, he estimated in 1936 the number to be about 15,000. Keeble said he alone wore out two or three tents preaching in Florida.

In April of 1936, Keeble was in Stephenville, Texas. In the first service, Keeble and William Lee were the only Negroes present. At no time were there present more than twenty-five Negroes. However, there were only 300 Negroes living in the whole city.

Keeble was next in Old Hickory, Tennessee, for a completely new experience. A big tent was set up, and the white church worked hard to have a great meeting. The Negroes just didn't show up, but large crowds of white people poured onto the tent ground. None were baptized. Keeble said he was approached many times afterwards in the large department stores in down town Nashville by white Christians who told Keeble, "You converted me in that Old Hickory meeting."

Keeble conducted a meeting later that year in Denver, Colorado. The meeting did not create a great stir as Keeble meetings generally did. But Keeble held one of his famous debates with a highly educated Negro preacher of the Seventh Day Adventist Church, by the name of Michael-John. The white Christians thought the church of Christ would suffer if Keeble met defeat at the hands of Michael-John. S. H. Hall advised by telephone it would be best for Keeble not to risk the debate. Keeble said, "I'm going to debate him." Marshall Keeble completely unharnessed the Seventh Day Adventist preacher after just one session.

During the debate, Keeble behaving like a perfect gentleman addressed his opponent as "Brother" Michael-John. Keeble explained, "The sectarians will push you into being as intelligent as they are." The Adventist preacher parading behind his degrees wanted to know "how Keeble learned so much Bible." He answered that one by demanding of Michael-John to show just one place in the Bible where the Seventh-Day Adventist Church was mentioned. Keeble told him, "Jesus nailed the Law of Moses to the cross and no man has the power to tear it loose." And Keeble added—"And you are a graduate of one of the biggest universities and don't even know it."

The debate was held on a Saturday and Keeble told Michael-John: "You are due to be dead right now—not here debating me—driving your car and working your servants." One session satisfied the Adventist preacher, and no one since, has advised Keeble not to hold a debate.

Keeble was called by the white churches in July, 1936, to Springfield, Missouri, to establish a Negro church. Although the audience grew until they reached 4000 the last night, only two Negroes were baptized and five white people. This would be a good place to say that no other preacher in the church of Christ has preached as long and to such huge audiences as Marshall Keeble. It is a safe observation to make that Marshall Keeble as a single gospel preacher has had more influence in direct contact with more people than any other gospel preacher in recorded history.

The balance of the 1930's were good years for Keeble jammed from January to December with gospel meetings and preaching appointments. When he showed up in Henderson, he was certain to turn up in Freed-Hardeman College for a chapel talk and always to the sheer enjoyment of the students. Keeble and William Lee were in Henderson for a meeting during the 1937 lectureship. Keeble mentions he met such good friends as H. Leo Boles and John T. Lewis.

How Keeble spent the winter months in Florida is best described by Keeble himself. He wrote the following account for the *Advocate* in 1937:

On February 9 we left Nashville to spend a few months in Florida. En route we spent one night at Chattanooga, and we found that church in a fine condition, and many white friends present to encourage us on our way. Alonzo Jones is doing a great work at Chattanooga.

We spent two nights at Atlanta. Brother A. C. Holt is loved by the church there. The West End church is still standing by the colored work. Some of them were present each night. H. Clyde Hale made a fine, encouraging talk while we were there. We also had a pleasant meeting with B. C. Goodpasture.

We spent one night at Valdosta, Georgia, and were greeted by a large audience. Brother Paul English is with this church. They are working in peace and love.

We began a two weeks' meeting at Tampa, Florida, resulting in eleven baptisms and four restorations. The house was packed. O. L. Aker is working with this church and in that section.

We spent two nights at Bradenton, Florida, where F. L. Thompson preaches. Two were baptized and the church encouraged. This church numbers more than eight hundred members, and it is only five years old. They have a splendid building paid for.

Next we visited the church at Gainesville, Florida. John Vaughner established this church while the white brethren supported him.

We visited a fine work which Brother Vaughner started at Alachua, Florida.

We were then in a three weeks' meeting at Pensacola, Florida, which resulted in sixteen baptisms and seven restorations. Junius Knight preaches there. The white brethren have stood by the work.

Next we began a meeting at Montgomery, Alabama, May 9. It closed with fifteen baptisms. Both white and colored enjoyed this work, and we are invited back by the white churches for 1938.

Pray for Brother William Lee and myself.

Keeble returned in 1938 for a meeting in Montgomery, Alabama. About a thousand persons attended each evening—half and half of the two races divided the tent. Later Keeble went next to Moundsville, West Virginia, where the largest crowds of his preaching season greeted him. Almost all were white. There were only fifty colored families in the city and few came. The white church at Wheeling, West Virginia, sent a truck load of Negroes for every service. Many white people who had never heard the pure gospel before came to listen to a Negro preacher, and never missed a service afterwards. Boyd Fanning who preached for the Moundsville church carried Keeble one day to Bethany, West Virginia, to visit the home and grave site of Alexander Campbell.

There is no end to the Keeble stories and they are mostly true. As the Apostle John said—"There are many other things that Jesus did that are not written in this book." And this is an accurate picture of the activities of this incomparable, diminutive dark-skinned man. He defies description. He excites admiration in a measure that could not be said of any gospel preacher in living memory. Floyd H. Horton of Birmingham, Alabama, described Keeble after he had conducted a four weeks meeting in that city baptizing fifty-five persons:

. . . I have never heard better preaching than Brother Keeble did during this meeting. He is so humble that it is an inspiration to be associated with him. To be around Brother Keeble you learn that you do not have to go around with your fist doubled up or a frown on your face in order to preach like Paul, nor do you have to wear a horse face and be a sissy in order to have the spirit of Christ. He is like a lamb in his dealings with his fellowmen, but like a lion when it comes to preaching the gospel and defending the cause, and this is the spirit of Christ. Those who come into the church under the preaching of Brother Keeble do not come in thinking that they are just swapping denominations, but they come in knowing and believing that the church of Christ is the only church that offers salvation to the world. The Woodlawn church supported this meeting, and we feel that the good the white congregation received from the meeting was worth many times the price of it.

One of his great meetings was conducted in Huntingdon, West Virginia. Joe Morris was preaching there at the time. Like Clyde Hale, J. W. Brents, and others, he was left speechless when he described what went on in the Keeble meeting. But he tried—

The Keeble-Lee meeting came to a close last night (August 22), with the largest crowd of the meeting. It was impossible for us to seat the audiences any night of the meeting. These brethren are at their best. I have never heard nor seen greater power in the pulpit. Sin was condemned, error exposed, and the church and Christ exalted to the heavens, and no man can do this with a greater degree of success than Marshall Keeble. I am sure there never was a better helper than William Lee. He is humble, faithful, and true. The result of the meeting was eight baptisms. Among the number were two preachers—one a Methodist, and the other a Baptist. The church was definitely established among the colored people, and the white church was greatly strengthened. All in all, this was a great meeting. May God speed the day when soft-soaping preachers and neutrals among the white preachers will have the courage to condemn sin and error and preach righteousness as does M. Keeble. We hope to have these brethren with us again next year.

The meeting that Marshall Keeble conducted at Ridgely, Tennessee, in 1939 is his most widely known meeting due to an unfortunate circumstance. Ridgely is located in the rich cotton belt of West Tennessee, heavily populated with the typical southern Negro. His education opportunities have always been few and poor. The success of Marshall Keeble in this small Tennessee town was like so many others. The people—white and black—poured out by the thousands—many were crossing the Mississippi River. Many came including the leading citizens of the community. A. O. Colley a well known white preacher came from Dyersburg every night to assist Keeble in the meeting. The story was told that so many of the young people attended the Keeble meeting that the street was roped off on Saturday night for a street dance to keep young people away from the meeting.

When the invitation was being extended at an evening service, a white man came forward. Keeble bowed to take his confessions. The man struck Keeble a staggering blow on the left side of his head with brass knuckles. Keeble was stunned for a moment but recovered. There is no truth to the story that Keeble suffered permanent damage to his hearing.

Why did the man commit the act? Some say that the white planters instigated the act. But the audience included many who were sympathetic with Keeble. What is closer to the truth is that some men got together with more religious prejudice than common sense. After a few drinks, a dare was made, some money offered, as the saying goes, and one person agreed to strike the blow. Anyhow the deed was done and the actual circumstances will never be known. The man died shortly afterwards. Some regarded it as an act of God! Keeble refused to prosecute the man even though leading citizens persuaded him to do so. The meet-

78

ing continued without other incidents. Keeble's conduct won him great favor with the whole community. Keeble is a wise man. He explained about his work all through the South—"You have to know how to work with both races. Tl e white people had control at that time and still do." The remarkable thing is that Keeble was injured only once. He said about preaching to the Negro in the presence of white people—"I had to know how to meet him or I'd get hurt."

The Keeble story of the 1930's must end at some place. Other than the unhappy circumstances at Ridgely, Tennessee, the year of 1939, found Keeble standing as a solid champion among his brethren. No person questions this, but the attempt to decipher this incomparable man goes on. He knows where his power to move people is. Like Paul—he has not been "ashamed of the gospel:" and the world has become a better place because Marshall Keeble has lived in it.

CHAPTER VII

The Christian Echo

The story of the remarkable growth of New Testament Christianity among the Negro race is far from being mainly the achievement of Marshall Keeble. The importance of G. P. Bowser in the Restoration Movement among the Negro people must not be under evaluated, or over shadowed by the work of Campbell and Womack. The influence of Bowser and his "sons in the gospel" strongly persists to the present. Bowser's reputation as an effective preacher and an able religious debater was enhanced by his being a pioneer in religious journalism and Christian education.

The influence of David Lipscomb's thinking was a powerful and pervasive influence on Campbell, Womack, and Bowser. Lipscomb had piloted the *Gospel Advocate* thirty-four years before Alexander Cleveland Campbell started the church in his home on Hardee Street, and the Nashville Bible School had operated ten years. What David Lipscomb accomplished with his pen, the school, and in the pulpit inspired the Negro Christians to do likewise.

A first attempt to start a religious journal for the Negroes like the *Gospel Advocate* was announced in 1902 in the *Advocate*. The prospectus was written by M. F. Womack, brother of S. W. Womack. The journal was named *The Minister's Bulletin*. Other than the announcement, the plans to publish the paper faded into oblivion. Only after Bowser began publishing *The Christian Echo* in 1903 was the hope to have a Negro Christian journal realized.

The history of *The Christian Echo* deserves telling. Its influence among Negro Christians for many years equals a similar influence the *Gospel Advocate* has among Caucasian Christians. In November of 1903, Bowser brought a small hand printing press into his home on Jefferson Street in Nashville. Shortly afterwards a one-page religious paper appeared bearing the name—*The Christian Echo*. While the name has gone unchanged, there have been several locations for its printing. For almost fifty years, Bowser kept the paper going. The *Echo* found a second home when the school was moved to Silver Point, Tennessee, from Jackson Street.

Bowser had a staff to assist him at Silver Point—the students and teachers. The type was set by hand. The little paper by then had advanced to four pages. One section was titled—"As The Editor Sees It"—written by Bowser. The second was titled—"Here and There" containing miscellaneous articles from different writers; and lastly, "Field Notes" sent in by preachers from the mission field.

In 1928, in telling the history of *The Christian Echo,* Bowser recalled the early efforts to establish the church in Nashville:

When Brethren S. W. Womack, A. Campbell, and a few others began a mission in a private home in Nashville, Tennessee, which resulted in the establishing of the Jackson Street Church, of which I soon became a part, we then did not foresee how far-reaching this movement would be. From this humble beginning of seven, who were full of zeal and faith, has grown a membership in Nashville around four hundred. A number of preachers and good church workers have been developed. Four meeting houses have been built in the city and another one is in progress. The influence of this work has permeated nearly every state in the union.

Harrison Ramsey is remembered in the Silver Point days as a good friend of *The Christian Echo* because his strong right leg powered the press. Bowser's daughters were also amateur printers. The paper then served a great need since it helped to draw the Negro Christians together and to put across to them the need of Christian education.

After Silver Point, Bowser moved to Louisville, Kentucky. By then he was able to equip a small printing office on Liberty Street. For a while Bible school literature was sold by the *Echo.* Keeble recalled that Bowser "made our song books which sold for twenty-five cents during revivals." The names of the associate editors and staff writers were announced April 20, 1928, in the paper—Alonzo Jones, Marshall Keeble, J. Hamilton, J. Hannon, and T. H. York. The paper had a hard go financially. Bowser supplemented the expenses from his meager income, and Fannie Bowser cooked and washed for money to help keep the paper going.

The next home for *The Christian Echo* of some duration was in Fort Smith, Arkansas, where in 1938 the Bowsers moved. The paper by then was issued twice monthly. The subscription rate was $1.00 a year or 50c for six months. The editors were G. P. Bowser, R. N. Hogan, and G. P. Holt. The staff writers were G. E. Steward, J. S. Winston, E. D. Phillips, Annie C. Tuggle, T. H. Busby, R. F. Nunley, and L. W. Kennedy. Bowser organized a school in Fort Smith named the Bowser Christian Institute. The students there were also active in the publication of the paper grown to eight pages. G. E. Steward was instrumental in persuading several churches to help support the *Echo* and the school. The Bowser Christian Institute closed in 1946.

Bowser and his family moved to Detroit, Michigan. Here he started another school also named The Bowser Christian Institute. The small school with its teachers was recognized by the Detroit Board of Education. The publication of the *Echo* continued as usual. Bowser's last home was in Fort Worth, Texas. G. P. Bowser loved teaching young men to preach the gospel, and he left this world doing just that.

When Bowser became ill in Fort Worth, Texas, he turned the publication of *The Christian Echo* over to his grandson, Marion V. Holt. He requested that G. E. Steward become the editor. Marion Holt decided to go to Southwestern Christian College to study the Bible. The *Echo* was published for a while by Eugene S. Smith of Dallas, Texas. R. N. Hogan was appointed the editor.

The publication of *The Christian Echo* finally became the responsibility of R. N. Hogan. A company was formed with Hogan as president, W. W. Godbolt, Treasurer, C. C. Wilson, Secretary, and J. S. Winston, Circulation Manager. At this writing, The Christian Echo Publishing Company is owned by R. N. Hogan.

However the efforts of the Negro disciples to organize schools and publish papers may be evaluated, their efforts in preaching fields may be examined with greater objectivity. The remainder of this chapter is designed to single out some of the leading Negro preachers and to provide some understanding—not only of the magnitude of their work, but also the great measure of success they enjoyed.

Bowser reported a year's work for the *Gospel Advocate*. This was a practice the *Advocate* editors encouraged.

During the year 1914 I preached in the following places: Nashville, Silver Point, Lebanon, Murfreesboro, Lancaster, Cookeville, Bellwood, Lewisburg, Belfast, Petersburg, Tullahoma, Manchester, Viola, White's Chapel, Brownsville, Germantown, Capelville, Franklin, Memphis, McEwen, Columbia, and Took Place, in Tennessee; Louisville, Ky., Luther, Okla.; Center Point, Ark.; Thyatira, Looxahoma, Belan, and Lyon, Miss. Number of sermons preached, 231; number of additions 72; amount collected, $436.21; traveling expenses, $127.46. There remains much land to be possessed. The great needs for successful field operations are more true able ministers, more zeal on the part of the church, and more financial support.

Bowser was the last of the "old timers" to pass. On Thursday evening, March 23, 1950, G. P. Bowser died. He remained active almost to the end of his life. The junior college in Terrell, Texas may be rightfully considered as the final outgrowth of Bowser to found a college among his people. The Bowser Memorial Fund has been set up in recent years to perpetuate his contributions to the restoration of New Testament Christianity.

In the following year of 1915, Aleck Campbell wrote a summary of his work for the *Gospel Advocate*. He sent in such reports from time to time:

During the year 1915 I preached under brush arbors, under the tent, on the riverside, in the courthouse yard (at Pulaski), in the streets, on the pike, in Christian meetinghouses, in Baptist meetinghouses, and in private homes in Tennessee; at Lewisburg, Center Star, Pleasant Union, Lebanon, Flat Rock, Cookeville, Algood, Centerville, Gray's Bend, Jackson Street, (Nashville), mission point in West Nashville, Hardshell Baptist meetinghouse in Nashville, Hillsboro Pike (near Nashville), North Nashville, Henry, Happy Hill, Bodenham, Dresden, Fosterville, White's Chapel, Long Branch (Lawrence County), Kayne Avenue (Nashville),—all in Tennessee; at Blackton and Santuck, in Arkansas, I married three couples and conducted five funeral services. Number of sermons preached, 275; number of additions, 65.

Campbell continued his work into the 1920's. Campbell was the father of eight children. One of his daughters, Alexine Campbell Page, taught with Bowser in the school at Silver Point. Campbell died in 1930 while living with his mother and oldest sister in St. Louis, Missouri.

Womack was the first of the pioneer Negro preachers to die. For the last two years of his life, illness slowly eroded his life away. He was confined to his home for the last ten months of his life. His suffering was great, but he never murmured. Old Brother Henry Clay spoke at the funeral. F. W. Smith and A. B. Lipscomb were present and spoke. A. M. Burton attended the services also. His funeral was conducted in the Jackson Street Church. The last sermons Womack preached were at Jackson Street. When he was so weak, he had to walk with a cane, Womack would often preach to the congregation sitting in a chair. David Lipscomb also sat in a chair while preaching the last years of his life.

Keeble recalled at Womack's passing that it had been Womack's delight while in town to visit the *Gospel Advocate* office where he was always welcome. Whenever he was puzzled over a passage of Scripture, he had a conference with David Lipscomb. After Lipscomb died, he was welcome to talk to A. B. Lipscomb, J. C. McQuiddy, F. W. Smith, and others. He was always ready to instruct his people, and he read the Bible daily. When he became too feeble to read, Keeble would read the Bible and the *Gospel Advocate* to him.

It is by now obvious that the preaching of the gospel to the Negro race is not primarily a Keeble story. There are also other splendid Negro preachers deserving of special attention in addition to Campbell, Womack, and Bowser. Although the roll call of the outstanding Negro evangelists that follows cannot be definitive, at least, partial honor is paid to a few of their number either advancing in age or deceased.

Outside of Nashville, the preaching of the gospel went slowly among the Negro race. John T. Ramsey is entitled to more than just an honorable mention. The *Gospel Advocate* contains a statement from his pen saying he was the only loyal Negro preacher in the enitire state of Texas about the time of World War I doing all he could to preach the gospel. Ramsey was joined in the scant years ahead by good Negro evangelists who "went everywhere preaching the Word" over Texas. An outstanding early Negro gospel preacher in Texas was T. H. Merchant.

An early Negro preacher whom few know about is S. R. Cassius. He is perhaps better known as the father of S. L. Cassius. Never at a loss for words, S. R. Cassius was given to speaking his mind in a very plain fashion. And David Lipscomb would publish what he wrote in the *Advocate*. Cassius was writing to the *Advocate* around the period of World War I. In one of his articles, Cassius was severely chastising his white brethren for their lack of interest in the Negro—"They tell me hell is paved with good intentions, and I fear its walls are papered with good resolutions, and if we could gaze up at its ceiling, we would find it frescoed with standing committees."

Booker T. Washington was revered by the Negroes of this nation for the leadership he provided. Cassius expressed an evaluation of the famed Negro's worth, and pointed out one ingredient that was lacking:

But amid it all, Booker T. Washington did not forget the fact that he was a Negro, and showed his great common sense by staying in the race, as far as social equality was concerned. It meant nothing to him. He made for himself a place in the whole nation, based upon manly achievement and not upon social or racial distinction. In other words, Booker T. Washington was in a class by himself. His race did not make him great, but he reflected greatness on the race. There can be but one regret; and this is, his great work was for the temporal rather than the spiritual uplift of the Negro race. Oh, that we could arouse a like spirit in the church of Christ for the spiritual betterment of the Negro race!

However Campbell, Womack, Bowser, and the early Negro preachers may be regarded, they clearly understood that the Negro's spiritual needs were of paramount importance. And they tried to do something about it.

Cassius was a persistent preacher of the gospel. The establishing and strengthening of the church in the Los Angeles area in the 1920's is largely due to his efforts. Cassius was in Denver, Colorado, in 1927, where he gathered twenty-six Negro Christians and started them worshipping.

The name of J. Hannon occupies an interesting place in church history. Hannon preached around Corinth, Mississippi, in the 1920's and 1930's. He worked in an iron foundry by day and preached the gospel nights and on Sunday's. In slack seasons and during vacations, he preached in Alabama and Arkansas. The fact that Hannon baptized the entire Johnson family which included Laura Johnson Keeble makes a good footnote to the Keeble story.

Dennis Matigan English earned a significant position in the ranks of gospel preachers of a past generation. He was born April 4, 1872, in Lewis County, Tennessee. English became a Christian in 1904, and started preaching in Hickman County, Tennessee. He became one of the finest preachers of his day conducting numerous gospel meetings and several religious debates.

Another fine evangelist responsible for starting and sustaining the work among the Negroes in Chattanooga, Tennessee, was Alonzo Jones. Bowser converted him. Alonzo Jones came from Mississippi to Tennessee. For a while he was an employee doing farm work for A. M. Burton. Keeble said Jones was one of the best "homemade" preachers in the 1920's. In 1935 Alonzo Jones wrote to the *Advocate* about a meeting in McMinnville, Tennessee—

On August 11, I began a tent meeting in McMinnville, Tennessee. It was attended by both white and colored. In spite of opposition, seventeen were baptized and thirteen restored. I thank God for the spirit of the white disciples toward the work among my people.

T. H. Busby towers among the finest Negro preachers past and present. He was a protege of G. P. Bowser and a student enrollee in the school at Silver Point where he also served as a music teacher. He did not show much promise as a preacher in his youth, but he was a great song leader. Keeble ran upon Busby while he was working with Bowser. Keeble described him as a "great and unusual singer, and now a 'number one' preacher." Today he holds as many meetings as almost any other two Negro preachers in the mission field.

There is one experience he must still remember while he was leading the song services for a Keeble meeting in Florence, Alabama. Each evening after service he and Keeble walked from the tent to their boarding place. Some young men blocked the sidewalk on one of the nights. One boy drew a pistol and fired off some shots. Keeble said he heard them "whistling" by his head. Keeble never missed so much as half a step. He pleasantly greeted them—"Good evening gentlemen" and walked on. Keeble's brethren had offered to drive him home after the services, but he declined their courtesy.

Keeble said he didn't believe the boys meant to harm him—just to frighten him. Keeble wasn't scared then and never ran in his whole life. Once he got a note from the Ku Klux Klan—"We will visit you at some late quiet hour of the night." Keeble lay awake waiting for them. They never came. Keeble didn't welcome such threats, but he wasn't intimidated by them. When he came to hold a meeting he stayed. If they cut his tent down, he put it back up. When doors were closed in one neighborhood, he moved a little further down the road and kept on preaching.

The son of S. R. Cassius won an important place among the Negro disciples for his Christian dedication. A. L. Cassius was born December 18, 1890, in Iowa. He was educated in Tuskegee Institute, and started preaching in 1932 in Los Angeles, California.

Not a great many years ago a new Negro religious journal was started and published by the Gospel Advocate Company through the interest of B. C. Goodpasture. It was named the *Christian Counsellor*. Marshall Keeble was the editor of the paper and A. L. Cassius served as the associate editor. The journal was short-lived due to lack of interest among the Negro Christians. *The Christian Echo* started first and continues to hold the interest of Negro Christians.

Marshall Keeble has a long standing acquaintance with the *Gospel Advocate*. He was writing for the paper when B. C. Goodpasture was still a boy. A lasting friendship was formed between the two in the early thirties. When J. T. Hinds, editor of the *Gospel Advocate* died in 1939, Leon McQuiddy was looking about for a new editor. McQuiddy was a taciturn man with little to say even to those closest to him. Leon McQuiddy and Marshall Keeble were good friends. And he would talk with Keeble about matters he wouldn't discuss with other people. His health was poor, and he told Keeble what worried him most was selecting the right editor for the paper.

Keeble told him—"B. C. Goodpasture is the right man." McQuiddy agreed but said he couldn't be pulled out of Atlanta. The right people must have applied the right kind of pressure. This is what Keeble advised his friend to do. There is no doubt B. C. Goodpasture made up his own mind about what to do; and like all the other great leaders of the church in Keeble's era, he has been an unfailing supporter of the Negro preacher—Marshall Keeble.

A. L. Cassius was an effective preacher and a great worker in the church. Cassius began preaching in 1932; he gave a good account of himself. A Negro Baptist church house in 1934, in Modesto, California, was the setting for one of Cassius' meetings. A royal welcome was given him by the Baptist preacher who said if "Brother Cassius could make any impressions upon those of his race, just to go right at it." It seemed that he had not been able to teach them; but after hearing Cassius, it was more than they could stand. Cassius was denied further use of the church.

Keeble has about as little prejudice in his nature as a man can have. But he is a prejudiced man when it comes to Luke Miller and John Vaughner. Keeble found Luke Miller in Decatur, Alabama, driving a truck for a furniture company. Luke came to the hotel around midnight to get Keeble to baptize him.

Keeble described the landlady's reaction when Miller wanted Keeble awakened: "What you want with him? He's gone to bed."

Miller told her, "I want to be baptized."

"Well, he won't baptize nobody tonight," and she ended the conversation.

After Luke became a Christian, he traveled with Keeble as his song leader. And Keeble said about Miller and his wife—"My, how they could sing!" Finally Miller got so many calls he began preaching. Keeble remarked that Luke preached more nearly like him than any other preacher he trained. Luke Miller baptized two hundred and eighteen in Corsicana, Texas. Keeble said—Luke and John jokingly said "they were going to pass by me in the number of converts." Keeble who had baptized two hundred ninety-six in the Bradenton, Florida, meeting told them—"You ain't never going to do that!" And they didn't.

Luke Miller was struck down in 1934 by a heart attack. The doctors dispaired for his life. His mother sent to Paris, Texas, for him, and Miller was brought to her home in Decatur, Alabama. Luke was at the height of his power. He was clean in his manner of life and held in honor by all who knew him.

When Miller was slowly recovering, the Sixth Street Church in Port Arthur, Texas, sent for him in the spring of 1935 to work with the Negro church after a great Keeble meeting. O. C. Lambert, white preacher, who was working with the Sixth Street Church, assisted Luke Miller who was still a sick man. He never fully recovered; but under the care of a heart specialist, he lived and worked for the Port Arthur Church about fifteen years and later moved to Bradenton, Florida.

Miller enjoyed deep sea fishing. He came off a stenuous fishing trip while preaching in a Miami revival. He was found later lying dead across the hood of his automobile which he was washing. Miller was living in his home in Bradenton, Florida, and devoting all his time to "meeting work."

Keeble never let it be known which preacher of whom he was the fondest—Miller or Vaughner; but he said about them "that he would make the fires and they would fan them." John Vaughner was a coal miner in Birmingham, Alabama, and a deacon in the Baptist church when Keeble "captured him with the gospel." Afterwards he traveled with Keeble studying the Bible with him. When Keeble preached in the big "coal and steel" city, he said "the coal miners were so sincere—reading their Bibles under the light of their helmets—smudging their New Testaments so they were hardly readable." When Keeble became president of the Nashville Christian Institute, Vaughner never missed an annual lectureship.

T. Q. Martin, beloved preacher of a past generation wrote to the *Advocate* describing a meeting of John Vaughner in McMinnville, Tennessee.

People came in truck loads and school bus loads for miles around in different directions. He was heard by as many white people as colored ones.

Many of the whites who heard him were practically nonchurch goers. Vaughner has a comprehensive grasp of Bible truth, and can make as clear the distinction between dispensations, covenants, shadow, and substance as any one whom I have heard. His father in the gospel, M. Keeble, says of him: "There are none among us more able than John Vaughner." He is soon to devote all of his time to evangelistic work, and will do a great work wherever he goes. His greatness is in his simplicity, and he delivers his message with great power.

Keeble laid the foundation for the Florida churches in the Tampa meeting. He established other Florida bridgeheads in St. Petersburg, Lakeland, and Bradenton. Then Vaughner and Miller took over the Florida church and built it from the ground up. Florida was Vaughner's mission field until his death.

Vaughner died in St. Petersburg, Florida. At the time of his death, he was giving all his time to holding meetings in widely separated places following the trial blazed by Marshall Keeble. Vaughner's funeral was conducted in a large tent especially set up to hold the vast audience that attended. Keeble was going to fly to St. Petersburg to preach his funeral and took sick at the Nashville Air Port. Keeble while reminiscing said Vaughner was more like him in holding meetings and baptizing people.

Another of Keeble's favorite preachers was O. L. Aker. He was an ordained Methodist preacher living in Florence, Alabama. Keeble wrote in the *Advocate* about Aker—

I took the truth and captured him from the Methodist and his wife also. He became a highly successful preacher. Although most of his work was done in Alabama, he worked some in Florida, Arkansas, and Texas, baptizing large numbers of people.

When Keeble started a new church, he had about twenty preachers he could move from one church to another to keep them going.

A famed Negro preacher and younger contemporary of Marshall Keeble is R. N. Hogan. James L. Lovell heard him in 1937 while Hogan was in a meeting in Denver, Colorado. Lovell was moved to say—

I consider Hogan the greatest preacher in the church. He . . . converts people of his race, but does more to stimulate the work in the white churches than a white minister would do. He is educated, has a brilliant mind, and preaches like one sent from God, and yet is as humble as Brother Keeble.

Lovell was not alone in his praise of Hogan. Rufus Underwood said—

Hogan is without a doubt one of the most powerful preachers in the brotherhood, and the secret of his success lies in the fact that he preaches without favor or compromise. Hogan conducted a meeting during 1936 in Langston, Oklahoma. Among those who responded to his preaching were the postmaster, a Methodist preacher, a Methodist steward, a Baptist songleader, five school teachers—one a principal and another a department head in the state college there.

Richard Nathaniel Hogan was born November 30, 1902, to Willie Hogan and his wife. The family moved from Hickman County, Tennessee, to Blackton, Arkansas. At the age of fourteen, Hogan went to Silver Point as a protege of G. P. Bowser who trained the boy to be a preacher. When Hogan turned seventeen, he had already baptized seventy persons. In the intervening years, Hogan has preached in widely separated places. He and Levi Kennedy evangelized the Southside in Chicago. Levi Kennedy is a widely celebrated gospel preacher who has also worked in the Nigerian mission field.

Over a six year period in the 1930's, R. N. Hogan started fifty new congregations and baptized more than fifteen hundred people. For several years Hogan has lived in Los Angeles where he now serves as minister of the church meeting at 57th and Figuero with a membership of more than seven hundred families. Hogan married Maggie Bullock of Mt. Pleasant, Tennessee, in 1920; and they are the parents of four children, eleven grandchildren, and twelve great-grandchildren.

Great leaders too often obscure the contributions that many talented people make to their advancement. A. C. Holt occupies a prominent place among the foremost Christian Negro leaders in the 1930's. Though the Nashville Christian Institute is rarely associated with his name, the school may have never emerged had it not been for A. C. Holt.

Holt was already established as an effective gospel preacher in the early thirties. Alonzo Williams introduced A. C. Holt in 1932 through the *Gospel Advocate*. Holt was born and reared on a farm in Marshall County, Tennessee, near Belfast. He was one of thirteen children. After finishing grammar school in Belfast, he walked seven miles to the Lewisburg, Tennessee High School to complete his education.

Since he was eighteen Holt has been active in church work. After moving to Nashville, he worshipped with the Jefferson Street Church teaching and served as Sunday school superintendent and later began to preach. When Alonzo Williams wrote the account, Holt had just completed a tent meeting in Lebanon, Tennessee, that had run for a month. Harry Pickup described Holt as a preacher in 1937: "A. C. Holt is one of the strongest and most able preachers in the brotherhood."

90

A brother, M. F. Holt, was equally devoted to the work of the church. He was born November 17, 1895, in Marshall County. In 1909, M. F. Holt was baptized by D. M. English. He married Thelma Holt, the daughter of G. P. Bowser. The Jefferson Street Church employed M. F. Holt as its first full time preacher.

A report of his work between January 1, and April 1, in 1942 was published in the *Gospel Advocate*. Holt was working with five different congregations in the Nashville area at that time. He visited in 590 homes and contacted 1,300 persons, distributed a total of 4,225 religious tracts. Nowadays we hear so much about personal visitation programs. This is an ancient story among the Negro disciples.

George E. Steward, an outstanding blind preacher, was born July 29, 1906, in Gail, Louisiana. Bowser baptized him March 15, 1931. He started preaching in Fort Worth, Texas, the same year. He was educated in the Training State School for the Blind in Austin, Texas. Since his conversion by Bowser, he has become one of the most effective preachers and leaders in the church today.

Bowser was living in Fort Worth, Texas, when he chanced to visit a Baptist meeting and ran into the blind preacher. With a New Testament especially prepared for the blind, Steward could read rapidly. Bowser was impressed by his sincerity and ability and called on him. And to Bowser's happy surprise it did not take too long to convince him. Almost at once Steward and his wife were baptized.

Thousands of Christians east of the Mississippi River remembered with delight William Lee. Marshall Keeble's songleader. Keeble ran into Lee while he was preaching in Los Angeles. Keeble's two favorite song leaders were Lonnie Smith and William Lee, and Keeble's audiences enjoyed their work. Both were good, but Keeble described Lee as a "professional." After William Lee left Keeble, he started preaching and so has Lonnie Smith. Both are still living.

The story of Marshall Keeble's preaching in the 1940's is tied in with his work with the Nashville Christian Institute. Keeble's meetings were, as in the past, phenomenal successes. The pattern was a little different since he was accompanied by the Nashville Christian Institute "preacher boys," and raised money to operate the school during the revivals.

However, two meetings in the early forties were different. All the white churches in Akron, Ohio, combined their forces in 1943 to hold a meeting for the Akron Negroes. A school building was engaged and thousands of white people came for miles around. Unfortunately the Negroes wouldn't attend the meeting.

Keeble moved next to Baltimore, Maryland, and stayed two weeks. The white Christians rented a large hall over a whiskey store and a pool room. But once again the Negroes showed up in scattered numbers. Keeble couldn't exactly explain why his race wouldn't attend. He raised the question that the school building and segregated hall served notice on the Negro that the white people were unwilling for them to use their buildings. Keeble added he had great success in the other large cities—Chicago, San Francisco, and Chicago.

All these cities had large concentrations of Southern Negroes. Few Negroes attended the Murfreesboro meeting, in the twenties—his birthplace; and they wouldn't come out hardly at all to the Old Hickory, Tennessee, meeting a few years back. But Keeble remembers one Nashville meeting in particular. After fame came to Keeble, Green Street in Nashville was roped off each night for a Keeble meeting and filled with chairs which were moved after each service. Thousands came—white and Negro. All who wanted to be Christians were baptized at the foot of Broad street in the Cumberland River by Richard Taylor.

The only way to end a "Keeble chapter" is to stop. The dictionary is filled with words not used before to describe what Keeble said and did, and it would take a mighty volume to tell it all anyhow.

CHAPTER VIII

That Man Keeble

Marshall Keeble has often been described as a humble man. "This is the lever that brings you up," Keeble explained. These words were spoken by a gospel preacher who felt the crushing blow of brass knuckles on his face, and heard bullets from a revolver whiz by his head. Keeble defies analyzing or stereotyping. He explained: "I have never taken care of the Bible. The Bible took care of me. I kept the Bible in front of me. You couldn't get to me for the Bible."

Keeble does not stand out in a crowd. He is small standing five feet and four inches. Most of his life he has weighed between one hundred and forty and one hundred and sixty pounds. However, he never seems self-conscious about his height. He wears his hair short, and there is a slight "cowlick" on either side of his forehead. The old superstition that a high forehead indicates a high level of intelligence, at least, holds in his case. He has an aquiline nose and fine drawn lips. His color is a smooth brown texture. For many years now Keeble has worn false teeth and a glass eye. He is a pleasant man to see at eighty-nine.

His carriage is erect and his dress is always modest and becoming. Keeble has a distinguished appearance with a face that is never seen unshaven. He never calls attention to his physical appearance. J. P. Sanders, Dean of George Pepperdine College, said white people often forget he is a Negro. Willie Cato said he and Keeble sat on the stage in an all Negro audience, and he found himself thinking—"Brother Keeble and I are the only two white people here."

He dresses conservatively and is attractive in appearance. At the Nashville Christian Institute Board meeting, Athens Clay Pullias always said: "Keeble, you are looking mighty sharp today." This was always to his delight. B. C. Goodpasture gives Keeble a new suit at Christmas time each year. The ceremony dates back to the Atlanta, Georgia, meeting more than thirty years ago. Keeble comes in just to pay a casual visit with a significant look on his face. Brother Goodpasture plays the game for a while. If he doesn't bring up the subject finally, Keeble will say—"I've come for my suit."

Keeble practices self discipline with common sense. Sumptuous meals have been prepared for him. He would eat a little from a dish or two and leave the rest untouched, or leave the table having hardly eaten a thing. He attributes his long life to such discipline. He use to warn John Vaughner who was a great eater. Vaughner would argue: "I'm not going to die in debt to my stomach; I've got to eat a lot to keep my strength up." Keeble told Miller and Vaughner they had to keep the Florida work going after his death. He said, "They are a longtime dead, and I have to take care of Florida."

A never failing courtesy marks the behavior of Keeble no matter what the occasion may be. He never attacks any preacher or person. Gentleness is the never failing hallmark of his success. Seldom has he ever raised resentment in his listeners. This is partially accomplished by his fine humor. Often he is stern in his reproof, but he never abuses his audience.

Keeble is respected as a preacher in a fashion that no other preacher in the church of Christ—living or dead—has enjoyed. Once he has preached in a city he never lost the love and affection of the church. So impressive have been the exploits of Keeble and the power of his sermons, endless discussions try to explain him. It is reasonably estimated that sixty-five percent or more of all Negro preachers trace their conversions to him.

Unlike famed evangelists such as Billy Sunday and Gypsy Smith, when Keeble converted a man, he was converted to Christ—not to Keeble. This does not imply that admiration for him is lessened. Many converted by him have been as fervent to preach the gospel as Keeble himself. Indeed he has a great following. He preaches what men believe who believe the Bible and they honor him for that.

Keeble's sermons could hardly be labelled as literary masterpieces or even very literate in spots. He explained—"I studied the Bible and I studied the people and how to relate the Bible to people. That's all." His speech is plain, and his parables and figures of speech possess a vividness that makes his ideas crystal clear in the flash of a second.

Keeble said: "When you are talking to common people, talk common language so they'll understand you." A secret of his

J. E. Choate, Marshall Keeble, B. C. Goodpasture

Governor Frank G. Clement, Marshall Keeble, Willie T. Cato

power with the spoken word lies in his unaffected use of the language. He never "puts on" to leave the impression that he has a formal education. He is far too intelligent for such a trick. His flow of language is perfectly natural, and that of a Southern Negro who lacks a formal education. He is no orator. And as such his sermons are a source of joy and great beauty resulting from a natural eloquence.

He is a man of superior intelligence. There is little question that he could have been taken in hand by knowledgeable people who could have helped him refine his language. What is perhaps most noticeable in his language is his frequent use of double negatives which tend to give a special emphasis to the point he is making. Keeble says "he don't" as a manner of speech habit, and so does many another person who has had the background to know better.

The contributions of Keeble to the church stem out of his preaching. His deep convictions grow out of an implicit faith in the Scriptures. No audience ever questions his sincerity. He stands for moderation and understanding. In his religious debates, he was firm but never rude. Keeble never talks to the church about social problems rising out of racial differences. On integration he once remarked, "I would rather get it slow than to get it wrong."

He preaches what he believes when he knows what he is saying is not popular, but his audience respects his uncompromising courage. His sermons are never outlined and defy analysis. But his audience never misunderstands him. In his sermons he shows a strong dignity that is tempered by his bearing of humility. He always has complete confidence and rarely makes any apologies for himself from the pulpit.

Keeble is at ease in the pulpit and speaks without effort. He is no gymnist and will speak for long minutes with his hands in his coat pockets. For the most part his gestures flow gracefully. He can be intense without being violent.

Keeble likes for his audience to "amen" his sermons. If they aren't forthcoming, he "amens" himself. He will tell an audience—"I've preached here half an hour and nobody's even grunted." He says the church of Christ has grown so nice they don't want excitement. He reminds his audience that the "church started off on Pentecost with a lot of excitement."

For more than fifty years Keeble has often preached three

times on Sunday and each night in the week. He never recalls that his voice ever failed him once. This is remarkable when it is remembered that Keeble spoke for decades without the benefit of a public address system. At the age of eighty-nine, Keeble may run on a track of thought he's traveled often, but he still commands his words and speaks with an ease which pleases his audience.

Keeble is a knowledgeable man. Like Will Rogers, he knows what's in the newspapers because he reads them daily. He listens to the radio and watches the news programs on television. But the Bible is his main book and he keeps a good Bible dictionary at his elbow. He is a regular subscriber to his favorite journals—*The Gospel Advocate, The Firm Foundation,* and *The Christian Echo.* He rarely uses Bible commentaries, but times were when he discovered a commentator had a clearer understanding of a verse, and would often touch on something that hadn't occurred to him. As Keeble says—"You don't have to drink in what he says."

The genius of Keeble is discovered in his power to grasp ideas and facts to help his audience. His ability to present a Bible doctrine through a simple story is a thing of joy and beauty. Keeble said of this—"I can't explain my gift no more than nothing. While some people studied the Bible to memorize it, I studied it to reach people." He understands the simplicity of his parables—"The Lord had gifted me somehow to answer these things, and a fellow can see his ignorance so quickly." He says: "Ignorance is an awful thing. It's bad though to be ignorant and not know it."

Keeble not only knows how to make a parable, he also knows the gospel is not always pleasant. He said his mother was kind and benevolent, and from her—"I've learned to talk rough to a man and make him like it." Keeble has baptized more sectarian preachers than any other preacher in the church of Christ.

What many a preacher has learned is that the parables of Marshall Keeble are "touch not, taste not, handle not" for the simple reason they are manufactured by him on the spur of the moment and bear forever his own name-brand. He says, "If I can't make a parable, I'm lost." Once preachers were trying out for a church, and each preacher in his sermon brought out—"now as Keeble says." A lady in the church said, "I've looked in my Bible, and I couldn't find where Keeble made these statements." Keeble never uses illustrations or examples—just parables. His language is his own, and his parables are peculiarly his own.

Keeble's logic is simply his use of stubborn facts. He describes himself: "I stand four-square on anything. I don't know how to use deceit. I have grown on facts. No man with any sense will deny a stubborn fact." Even when his hearers don't agree with him they don't misunderstand him. In a meeting at Jackson Street Keeble commented—"I'd rather be standing on God's word than on the heavens and the earth—for the heavens will pass away; but Jesus says 'My words shall not pass away.'" There is one statement he has made above all others—"The Bible is right. You go home and fuss all night. The Bible is right. You can walk the streets and call Keeble a fool, the Bible is right. You can go home and have spasms, the Bible is right."

The person who sees only the "comic" in Marshall Keeble is naive. This is a charitable observation. Whoever gets the notion that Marshall Keeble has gone through life "clowning" should take a deeper and closer look at the man. He explained the value of his humor:

I am a little funny or comical, but it's been a joy to me. It's kept my enemies from bothering me. I have carried along a lot of humor just to flavor my message. You can put too much flavor in anything. Does me good sometimes to go home and lay in the bed and laugh at myself. People are so easy to teach if you know how.

Keeble is a complex man. He never uses humor just to be funny and never tells a "canned joke." There is a fresh originality in his humor because it is always self-conceived. And not until he has delivered his line does he realize the impact his words have made on the audience. Often times he will laugh with the audience at something funny he has said. No one has the impression that Keeble is not serious even when his wit has his audience almost "rolling in the aisles." Though he is an aged man and much of his wit falls into old patterns, there are still sparkling moments when the creative brilliance of his wit shines through.

His favorite form of humor is always directed at the situation not the person. For many years Keeble made an annual visit to the Tennessee State Prison to preach to some two thousand inmates always to their delight. His irrepressible humor would be brought into play. "I make them feel like they're just visiting—that they're not in prison. I carry the sunshine to them. I go into the crooks and corners. I call names sometimes. God deliver me from a hintin' preacher." The prisoners would get a little peeved when Keeble would say—"These guards are your friends." Then they would both laugh. The prison authorities told him—"Prisoners talk about you until next year rolls around."

Keeble uses a form of sarcasm that is seasoned with his wit and humor so that even his victims feel no malice. Keeble says: "You can call a man a liar if you know how to call him a liar. If you don't know how to do it, I'd advise you it's best to leave him alone."

Marshall Keeble is a fine gentleman with an indescribable gentle courtesy. He would tell this story:

I had a mule once I used to drive and he taught me how to be a gentleman. If I came into the stable and didn't speak to him like I ought to, and if I didn't hurry up, he'd kick me out of that barn.

See he didn't know but what somebody was going to hurt him. He'd just whale away. I'd say—"Gee" and "Haw." He knew my voice—that's all there was to it. But I had to speak and use good manners. When you came in that barn you'd better introduce yourself. I've avoided many a kick from that mule and people by kindly speaking to them.

Keeble never questioned the sincerity or honesty of his audience, but he knew the Bible could be misunderstood. To make his point, Keeble would tell this parable—

"Take the biggest elephant there is—standing right in the middle of the railroad track. He's going to butt the fastest train. He's just as honest as he can be, but he doesn't know you can be honestly wrong. Just as serious as he can be, but he doesn't know you can be seriously wrong. Just as serious as he can be, but he's seriously mistaken. I admit his strength, but his judgment is bad standing right in front of the 'Dixie Flyer.'"

Keeble had many a debate about "nobody getting religion." They wanted to know—"What's become of those 'old time people' before you got here that you say never 'got religion.'" That came up in the Bradenton, Florida, meeting. There was a large cemetery on a hill near the tent.

"Why, right up there where you laid them. They ain't got up yet. You want to know where they are going? I know your preacher done told you your mama went to heaven early this morning."

Then Keeble would lower the boom: "Your mama didn't even get in heaven late this afternoon. I don't mean no harm." Keeble would add: "Your mama has got to be judged in the last judgment day." Before he would finish everybody would be smiling. Keeble would end up baptizing the "angry man who said Keeble's preaching my mama to hell."

Marshall Keeble explained his humor: "I learned to make my

teaching instructive and entertaining. Here comes the truth and you slap the plaster on him. Humor doesn't destroy sincerity." He knew the preaching of the gospel could be both "bitter and sweet." If you give a man some medicine that'll do him good—shake it and take it quick! Don't set around fussing about a pill. Get off all that sweetness; it's one of the bitterest things you ever ran across."

He never minded flying on the big commercial carriers after his first flight from Los Angeles to Nashville. When James O. Baird, President of Oklahoma Christian College and Dr. George Benson of Harding College were accompanied by Keeble to raise money for Baird's school, they had a time persuading Keeble to ride in Dr. Benson's private plane. Finally he told Keeble: "I've got a World War II fighter pilot driving this plane." Keeble said—"Let's get on—he's carrying a fighter."

Keeble's humor is "homemade" and some of his expressions are classic. He is blessed with wealthy friends. He has raised countless thousands of dollars for worthy Christian causes. Such a statement he often makes —"I'd rather have friends than money." After a brief pause, he concludes—"Provided my friends have money."

Keeble had many a religious debate—or discussion with sectarian preachers who came to his meetings and challenged him from the audience. The secret of his power cannot be confined to his humor or any other single quality. Undoubtedly what contributed to the high excitement and vast audiences who attended Keeble's meeting in the twenties and thirties were his impromptu religious debates. Most Negro preachers were little better educated than he and were fully persuaded their doctrine could more than match Keeble's. In this they were seriously mistaken.

He conducted one formal debate in 1928 with D. T. Haywood a Holiness preacher from Indianapolis, Indiana. Will T. Cullum served as Keeble's moderator. After just one night of debate before a large Negro and white audience, Keeble said Haywood "was called home and could stay no longer." A Keeble debate was as unique as the man himself. No preacher ever conducted a gospel meeting like he did. Keeble invited any body in the audience to challenge what he was preaching and many did. He said "they kept up a lot of fussing and stopping me to ask questions."

A Keeble debate ran somewhat in this fashion. He was attacking the use of the organ in Christian worship. A challenge from the floor came—"My pastor can meet you on that. He can prove it. I've seen him debate it."

Keeble responded, "All right, bring him down."

"I'll bring him tomorrow night."

Keeble would give him the floor.

He would warm up to his task. "You can stack organs from here to heaven and they won't keep you from being saved. Organs won't keep you out of heaven."

Everybody would say "Amen."

Then Keeble got up. And with his first sentence, everything the man said went out the window—"I'm not fighting stacking organs. I'm fighting playing them."

Keeble said one of his main choir leaders was baptized that night. Often after such a debate, Keeble said he felt so sorry for the preacher with his members coming forward. Keeble said— "Sometimes I'd ask him to get up so his members would have a place to set." In an after thought, he added—"I've cleaned many a fellow!"

Keeble always gave his opponent all the time he needed. Then he got up and the preacher started "burning." He'd sit down and want the floor again. Keeble would say: "No you've had plenty of time. I didn't ask you to sit down, now, don't bother me. I'm just answering some questions you left up here."

"Well, I just want to . . ."

"No, you sit down. You been up here forty-five minutes. I didn't bother you." Keeble said, "I was ruining him and winning all the time."

And he was always so nice to his opponents—"Here's an honest man—if he wasn't honest, he wouldn't come up here. He's honest and wants the light turned on. I'm going to turn on the light." The crowd would laugh a little bit and he'd laugh. First thing you know I'd have him "burning again:" He'd want to get up again and answer me. "Now when you were up here, I didn't bother you." Keeble always won his debates. When he would arrive in a large city for a meeting, none of the Negroes were members of the church of Christ. They were favorably impressed with his conduct and said: "Keeble was so fair and treated our preacher so nice, but our preacher acted so bad."

101

However, Keeble sometimes lost his audience in his debates and had to go back and get them. He would say when misunderstood—"I didn't mean to say that. I wouldn't offend you for nothing. I'd apologize—then win both him and the audience. You can lose the debate and still be right. That's when you lose your audience."

Many a Keeble meeting set a whole city in an "uproar." The interest grew out of the impromptu debates. Preachers challenged Keeble from the floor. He took them on right then when they were "red hot." "Come up here and prove your point."

"I can do it all right," the preacher would say, and Keeble would hand him his Bible when he came to the pulpit.

Or Keeble would say—"Here's a gentleman who can prove I'm not right."

Or he would say, "If you can prove there's a Baptist Church in the Bible, come back tomorrow night and prove it."

"I can prove it," came the rejoinder, and you never saw such a crowd that would be there the next night.

Keeble would ask him to name just one place where a Baptist Church was mentioned. And he couldn't do it. Keeble explained—"You got to have facts or somebody will knock you down."

It took a long time for Keeble's opponents to learn the best way to answer him was to leave him alone. Their preachers who had met him in debates sent word on down—"Don't bother him. It'll just make his meetings grow—leave him alone." Keeble said in his early days one of the "poor things" (preachers) would jump me, and I'd have to shoot one or two every night with the gospel.

He explained his art of religious debating. "You've got to know how to skin a man without making him holler. You just have to know how to do it and in a way that's pleasant. You set him to crying and everybody sympathizes with him." He told about a debate he once heard. The church of Christ preacher's opponent couldn't answer him and he started crying. He got the sympathy of the people. The preacher didn't know when to quit beating him and the more he cried, the more the people sympathized with him."

The worst mistakes an educated preacher ever made in attacking Keeble was to back up his arguments with his degree rather than the Bible. Sometimes Keeble would rebuke his audience for their failure to obey the gospel. "You don't have the courage.

102

There's your preacher out there showing I am right. He's not bothering me. Their preacher just standing there laughing. Then he'll come forward and later tell his parishioners—'I wouldn't a done it, but he's right. I knew it soon as I heard it.' " Sometimes the town preachers would come out and listen from the outskirts of the crowd and Keeble would say—"You out there behind those piles of cross ties! I see you out there hiding behind a bush! That's how you been telling what I said. I know you are out there now. You come right up here and tell me where I am wrong." Keeble always had his tent grounds well lighted for the light served as an exposure and protection.

His arguments were never complex or subtle. They were plain and he meant for them to be understood. Baptism was often a subject for controversy. And he would say in few words so much. "If you get saved before you hit baptism—you're too fast. God never dry cleaned a man dry since his Son died on Calvary. You put God in the dry cleaning business when you have him saved before baptism." Keeble would have to wait until people would get through laughing.

Keeble could fashion a parable out of the most unlikely subjects such as "cylinder oil." The Methodist would jump Keeble when he preached against "sprinkling" for baptism. He would use the service station attendant who wanted to know if the motorist wanted, "light, medium, or heavy" oil. Keeble said that's how the Methodist were—so accommodating. "They wanted to know if you wanted it light, medium, or heavy (sprinkling, pouring, or immersion)?" He would be complimenting denominational practices and "skinning" their preacher all the while.

There was no end to Keeble's "home spun" parables. He said to wash something you've got to use something else in the water. In baptism, something else is used—that's the blood of Jesus. He says when you carry your clothes to be baptized, you put in Tide detergent. Keeble explained the "water and blood" are still together. "You got to come here to have your sins washed away." He explained such illustrations—"It was simple things like this that made it interesting to the audience. They had never heard it taught that way. The doctrine of Christ was so new it was excitable."

Keeble had a way of answering his "shouting religious neighbors" so as to quiet them. The preacher of the Primitive Baptist Church would say that mine is the oldest church—it was here "be-

103

fore the clouds were flying." Keeble would say, "That's too soon. When Christ came to set up his church the clouds were already flying. You are too early." Keeble would have to wait until the audience finished laughing.

When the sectarians got on to Keeble, he could no longer use their preachers as bait to create excitement. He would rebuke a "Holy Roller" preacher. "Here you talk about speaking in tongues, and you can't even speak the English language very well. You can't show me where the apostles were down rolling waiting for the Holy Spirit to come. Then he would start working on the "Holy Roller" preacher and getting the sympathy of the audience: "He ought to be ashamed of himself—having you down there rolling and waiting for the Holy Spirit."

How Keeble would work on the "mourner's bench!" "You can't have a 'mourner's bench.' Peter told Cornelius to stand up when he tried to get down, and Ananias made Paul stand up." Keeble always drew a laugh when he told about how long that mourner's bench would have been at Pentecost when three thousand obeyed Peter. Keeble said—"You just have to wash him to get all of that out of his mind—just brain wash him."

Keeble stated "When you hit the music question you hit all the sects. Make a drag through there—you got them all." He would say: "What would Paul looked like with a guitar around his neck walking down the streets of Jerusalem! Then he would say: "You would have to imagine it, because it's not in the Bible." He would have to stop talking so they could enjoy themselves. Keeble added, "You never heard such laughing."

Keeble said—"I don't believe in sugar-coating the truth—only seasoning it with salt." His converts sometimes created a lot of strife among the Negroes. One would be baptized and go over to the Baptist Church and just raise sand saying—"Everybody's going to hell!" Keeble remarked about such converts—"Don't know how to polish nothing. Then they'd want to fight. Don't tell me my mama is going to hell!"

There were occasions when Keeble almost got caught in this trap.

"Where's my mama?" an angry listener would demand.

"I don't know your mama. I'd get out that way. I knew what he meant. I wasn't talking about your mama. I don't even know her. I couldn't be talking about her. That's how I

104

dodged him." They were puzzled by such answers from Keeble, but they were comforted. At least, they were certain he meant no personal injury.

Another "Keeble classic" happened in a California meeting. A young white man got up and challenged Keeble.

"You have spoken about every other church, now what about mine?"

Keeble said—"I don't know what church you are a member of."

The young man responded—"The Latter Day Saints."

Keeble shot back—"You're too late!"

"The next night he was up a little closer, and here he comes to be baptized," Keeble said.

The young man told Keeble—"I don't stay in anything that is too late." Keeble often related the incident—"Lot of you sitting out there are too late."

There is no end to the Keeble stories. Put Keeble on a platform in a large Southern city with thousands of people sitting and standing. Words can't go on paper to describe the excitement and high emotions attendant to a Keeble meeting. And listening to Keeble's voice was like listening to a great symphonic orchestra that touched and stirred the deepest soul of man.

> Beauty through my senses stole.
> I yield myself to the perfect whole.

Marshall Keeble is "wise as a serpent and harmless as a dove." He knows how to handle his large Negro and white audience with a consummate skill that is a marvel to behold. He always identifies with his own race. Most of his years spent in preaching the gospel has been directed to his own race; but white people have flocked by the thousands to hear him. "He shot at the Negro, but it always back-fired on the large white audience." He is perhaps the only living evangelist among the churches of Christ who commands great audiences with the simple announcement that "Marshall Keeble will speak here tonight."

Keeble never objected to preaching to segregated audiences. This intelligent man knew that he could preach all over the South in this atmosphere. He held a meeting in Memphis, Tennessee, sponsored by the Union Avenue church of Christ. On the first night of his arrival at the tent, a rope was stretched down the middle. He asked the white preacher who put that rope up. If he knew he didn't tell Keeble who said—"I can't preach over these ropes." He took them down and put them under the pulpit with neither anger nor arrogance. Keeble never found where the apostles preached over ropes.

Keeble accepted the prejudices held against the Negro race. He never once in his life preached about the injustices suffered by his race. And never once did he take his text "God hath made of one blood. . . ." Keeble usually praises his audiences, or some efforts of the white people who helped make the meeting a success. He meant to be friendly with his audience, but he always stood a little apart from them.

In the 1920's and 1930's, Keeble preached before large audiences of uneducated Negroes. To them, Keeble also was uneducated, but they were impressed that he was respected by the finest white people in the community. All sensed that Keeble appealed to everyone because of the goodness of his life.

He is a master of applied psychology. A source of his humor lies in his keen analysis of both the Negro and Caucasian. Until recent years, he seldom glanced at the white audience who listened in rapt attention and watched his every move. R. N. Hogan summed up what Keeble was doing:

> He said everything he could say about those Negro Baptist and Methodist. He showed them how they had been misled by the "blind guides" called "reverends," and "presiding elders." All the time he was talking, his eyes were on the Negroes. In the process the Caucasians who were laughing at the Negro Baptists and Methodists finally realized that Keeble was exposing their erroneous practices, also, because they were Baptist and Methodist.

Keeble said about white preachers: "A sectarian will come to hear me quicker than he will you all. He'll just laugh at me and get mad at you. Before it's over with, he's crying, because he's so sincere."

The question is often asked "What does Keeble believe about segregation or desegration, or something or other?" The answer is simple—Keeble believes in preaching the gospel. There is a rock in Tuscumbia, Alabama, once used as an auction block for selling slaves. Keeble said he got on that rock and preached the gospel. He has often been told—"You have done more to break down religious prejudice than anybody else."

Keeble never preached a sermon on segregation. "Some of my Negro brethren," Keeble said, "couldn't think of nothing else.

You don't win the Negro, just make him mad, and turn the white people against you." But Keeble knew how to work on a white audience without ever touching them. He began with Peter's net and God's order: "What God hath cleansed, that call not thou common. God doesn't want you to call a man unclean because he's black. God created him. Don't you call him common or unclean." Keeble said the white people would "amen" what he was saying. He would press the point. "Call no man common so he can't accept the gospel; Peter had been baptized with the Holy Spirit, and Peter's heart was just full of prejudice." Wisdom is justified of her children, and she never had a more apt pupil than Keeble. Keeble said when he made a "drag" with that gospel net that got everybody.

He had a way of making the white man see himself. Often he would rebuke the Negro with the palm of his hand and back-slap the white audience. "Negro can't borrow anything up North. Come down South, go to the back door with your hat in your hand and they'll give you anything you want. The white man in the South wants you to respect him. Up yonder they ain't caring nothing about respect. They're hard boiled."

Marshall Keeble's life has been threatened on several occasions including bodily injury. His courage was never reckless but controlled by his wisdom. No matter what the indignities were that he suffered at the hands of Negro or white, he remained calm and courteous. He baptized a Negro woman once in Duck River in Tennessee. Her husband said he would kill Keeble and waited on the bank with a shotgun. Keeble went right on into the water and baptized her and the husband later.

In a West Tennessee town, a white man threatened Keeble: "You preach like this anymore, you'll leave town or we'll kill you."

Keeble answered: "I kissed my wife before I left Nashville, Tennessee. My Lord died for me, I'd just as soon die for him in Lexington, Tennessee, as anywhere else." That concluded the whole matter.

Nor were the Negroes always friendly. While in a meeting in the early part of 1933, in Sarasota, Florida, the sectarians put up a hard fight against Keeble. They threatened to burn his tent, including other veiled threats of one kind or another. Fifty-two were baptized during the meeting.

Keeble may lack a formal education but he is a man with rare talents. He remains even a delightful enigma to himself. All of his life he has strictly identified with his own race, and he is proud of their accomplishments. But his associations with white people has an unparalleled uniqueness. Keeble said about them—"There's one thing about the white Christian, he'll help any race that'll obey the gospel." The white people would tell him when he came to a destitute field: "Keeble, we got a brand new tent." And the white people get more out of the meeting than the Negroes.

Paul Tucker tells the story, that when he was a high school student, Keeble was running a meeting in Dickson, Tennessee, at the same time the white people started theirs. A white elder was not present for the service in his own congregation. They learned he was attending Keeble's meeting. White people learned the lesson much more quickly than it took Negro sectarian preachers to learn that it was not best to debate Keeble. The white churches just never ran a gospel meeting when Keeble was in town because most all the white Christians without apologies and a good number of the Negro population went out to hear Keeble.

By the middle thirties he was pretty generally known. He would be out in Oklahoma somewhere with Lonnie Smith. Keeble said: "We'd pull up to a filling station. The attendant would say—'How are you boys?' Calling us boys. 'What are you doing here?' 'You a preacher?' 'Are you Keeble?' He would fill the tank and say—'Go ahead you don't owe me nothing.'"

Lonnie Smith would ask him—"Who is it Brother Keeble that don't know you?"

Keeble would say—"I don't know. I drove in there to get gas—didn't know I had a brother here."

As Keeble often describes himself—"Just a simple man that didn't go to college to get his brain expanded." But to all who know Keeble or about Keeble never cease to be amazed at "that man Keeble" who has never suffered with a "swelled head."

CHAPTER IX

The Nashville Christian Institute

Marshall Keeble's interest in Christian education goes back to the little school on Jackson Street. He served as treasurer for the Silver Point School, and showed an active interest in the Nashville Christian Institute in the early 1920's when the school existed only as a dream. After fame came to Keeble in the 1930's, his presence on Christian college campuses excited students as no other speaker could. This included the governor of the state or whoever the visiting dignitary might be.

Keeble spoke to a chapel audience at Abilene Christian College in 1935, and wrote about the experience—

The boys and girls are wonderfully trained for future service in the church. I hope some day to see a school for our colored boys and girls because it is badly needed. Our young preachers are doing fine when we consider that they have no place to be trained by such godly men as Ijams, Hardeman, Cox, and Armstrong. I pray that these men may live long.

It is a formidable challenge for the most talented speaker to address a college audience. Since the 1930's Keeble has spoken to college audiences in the nation's largest cities to the sheer delight of academicians as well as students. For decades Marshall Keeble has been the star attraction on the annual lectureships of the Christian colleges.

The last lines of the last chapter of the story of the little Christian school that was organized in 1907 in the Jackson Street Church are now being written. The doors of the Nashville Christian Institute, which embodied those early plans for a Christian school for Negroes, closed in the spring of 1967. The dreams of G. P. Bowser, S. W. Womack, and Aleck Campbell to start a school like David Lipscomb's Nashville Bible School strongly persisted. The Silver Point School grew out of the desire of a small group of men to elevate a new generation of young Negroes through spiritual and academic training. The passing of the school at Silver Point was a great disappointment to G. P. Bowser and his associates. But they were accustomed to set-backs and failures.

The Silver Point School failed because it lacked a well-trained Negro faculty and adequate financial support. The earliest efforts of the Caucasians to help educate the Negro race stressed the industrial aspects of education. This practical approach created immediate benefits for the Negro race just after the Civil War. Little thought was given to provide a liberal arts education for them because of the impracticability of such a program. However, time has changed this attitude.

Annie C. Tuggle wrote in 1924 to the *Gospel Advocate*:

> It is impossible to estimate the far-reaching good that has been made possible through the kindly generosity of the white race in helping the black race. Fisk University, Tuskegee Normal Institute, Tennessee State Normal, and other similar institutions of learning stand out as a memorial of the love and sympathy the one race has for the other. But this sort of training alone—of the head and hand—is not sufficient.

The story of Christian education among the Negro is known only in fragments, but the details are present in an unbroken continuity to the present. The people who got the Silver Point School going also organized the Nashville Christian Institute. Bowser went to Louisville, Kentucky, after the Southern Practical Institute closed in the early part of 1920.

The present Nashville Christian Institute was born in 1920 and showed little promise until 1939. After A. M. Burton's Southern Practical Institute failed to go, he turned his attention to David Lipscomb College. He became a member of the David Lipscomb College Board during the A. B. Lipscomb Administration.

P. H. Black, who bricked the school at Silver Point, was joined by J. R. Holmes, and Dr. J. D. Fowler in purchasing a seven acre tract of land, June 15, 1920, near Fisk University with an old twelve room brick building that had once been a plantation home in the ante-bellum South. They planned to start a school in the building as soon as possible and named the prospective school—The Nashville Christian Institute.

The property was purchased for $7,000. A thousand dollars was paid down with six other one thousand dollar notes due annually with the stipulation that the interest would be paid semi-annually. For three years they met their obligations and spent an additional $2,000 repairing the buildings and putting a wire fence around the acreage. P. H. Black wrote:

> We are but few in number, and we are having a hard pull, but by the help of God, we have shouldered the responsibility to erect and maintain an institution which means to us that men can be better educated along this line; we must admit that the colored people need it.

Plans were made to open the school in 1923. Purchases were

Marshall and Laura Johnson Keeble

Mary Campbell's speech class on WLAC
at Central Church of Christ

made of blackboards, seats, desks and other school supplies. However, their hopes were immature. The school didn't open that year and seventeen years passed before it did. Although G. P. Bowser had moved to Louisville, Kentucky, his interest in the new school was as lively as ever. He commented in 1924:

> The one thing needed, and I might say badly needed, is a stronger force of preachers—efficient preachers; intelligent preachers; earnest consecrated preachers. I am sure this cannot be accomplished without Christian schools, and I do not infer that schools can make preachers. I abhor the idea of school as a preacher manufacturer. But I heartily endorse the idea of a school to train, prepare, and educate those who are inclined and desire to preach and teach the word. Several efforts have been put forth to establish and maintain a Christian school, but so far, we have not succeeded. Our present effort to establish the Nashville Christian Institute bids fair to become the most successful of all our efforts.

In this respect, Bowser is somewhat of a prophet since the Nashville Christian Institute was the first of two Negro schools to open. David Lipscomb's thought is clearly mirrored in the statement of Bowser's philosophy of Christian education.

The hope to open the school was kept alive in the 1920's. The indebtedness was retired. Then the "Great Depression" in 1929 threw the nation into economic paralysis. P. H. Black and others wouldn't willingly give up. Black gave the first dollar toward the new school and never missed a year giving thereafter. The people interested in starting the Nashville Christian Institute saw their way clear in 1939. Other than meeting sporadically in the old Heffernan home to hold Bible classes from time to time to keep tax free possession of the property, little else was done.

In 1939, the city of Nashville initiated negotiations for the Heffernan property as the location for the Ford Green Elementary School. In exchange for the Heffernan property, the city gave the Board of Trustees of the Nashville Christian Institute $11,500 and the old Ashcraft City School Building located at 801, 24th Avenue North. The Nashville Christian Institute moved into the abandoned Ashcraft building and plans were made to begin operating a school.

The school opened its doors for students in 1940. The prospects for a good school were dim in the early stages. The first students were grown men and women. Holt and his associates did what they could to get students. The Nashville Christian Institute was a night school at first. The curriculum met the needs of adults whose educational opportunities had been limited.

The catalog described the purpose of the school and course of

112

studies—"As a means to an education in its highest and noblest aspects, the Bible the 'Book of God,' stands without a rival." To study the Bible was the reason that brought the school into existence. In addition to the Bible, courses in English, public speaking, history, and mathematics were offered. A vocation department offered training in wood work, pressing, and dry cleaning. The curriculum also included home economics, music, voice, and a glee club.

In addition to A. C. Holt and P. H. Black, J. C. Comer, Dr. J. D. Fowler, and J. R. Holmes deserve special notice. It was through their interest that the Nashville Christian Institute became a living reality. Dr. Fowler first learned that the city wanted the Heffernan property. He and A. C. Holt worked out the business end of the deal. J. C. Comer ran a moving business in Atlanta, Georgia. J. R. Holmes was a land holder and a successful farmer. The late Robert Campbell, son of Aleck Campbell, was a member of the Board of Directors. His father had baptized him in 1907 during the Kayne Avenue mission meeting. Campbell was a successful Nashville undertaker, and served as the school's first treasurer in 1939.

Marshall Keeble was also a member of the Board of Directors and served on the Executive Board of the Nashville Christian Institute. He spent little time with the school at first since he was away in meetings. Another person deserving mention is M. F. Holt. He was interested in the new school and helped out in whatever way he could.

The school at first was not accredited. Lacy H. Elrod who was Supervisor of the Department of Accreditation with the Tennessee Board of Education, is especially deserving of praise. He arranged for the school to be accredited by the Tennessee Board of Education. Being a trained school man, Elrod knew what needed to be done. A general appeal went out to church members for funds to purchase the necessary school equipment required by the State Board. Their requests were generously met. The school opened as a fully accredited elementary and high school in 1942.

That the school was accredited in the first place stemmed out of the interest that influential people had in the school. Eight years after the school's beginning, W. E. Brightwell summed up the actual circumstances:

113

The institute is an orphan on our doorsteps, without the benefit of a basket, to say nothing of ribbons, buttons, and bows. Physically it has been crudely pieced together out of second-hand salvaged materials. Discarded equipment has been used with gratitude. Boarding students have done most of the construction. Such conditions have developed the home variety of ingenuity on the part of teachers and students. The boarding students actually dug out a basement area for their living quarters.

After the school was organized, children were entered on all grade levels. The first children to attend the school were Robert Woods, James and Lewis Williams.

When the Nashville Christian Institute became an accredited school in 1942, it was the only existing elementary and high school among the Negro disciples organized to give students the benefit of a Christian education. A. M. Burton took a lively interest in the school and decided to support it. Marshall Keeble succeeded A. C. Holt as the head of the Nashville Christian Institute. Holt's title had been superintendent. Keeble was the first Nashville Christian Institute school head to wear the title of "President."

At the time Keeble was elected to the post, the objection was raised that he lacked the formal education to qualify for the post. Burton told the Board and Keeble that the Tennessee Board of Education had assured him that "you don't have to know anything to be president of a school. Just the teachers must have degrees." Keeble told the story at Freed-Hardeman College during a lectureship. President H. A. Dixon jokingly told Keeble that statement gave him a lot of personal comfort.

A. M. Burton made a brief speech the year of the accreditation of the Nashville Christian Institute that has had far reaching historical implications on church history and gives a rare insight into the heart and mind of this man:

I feel much encouraged over the number present here this afternoon. No one can appreciate Brother Keeble more than I can, I don't believe, since I have been working with him in a small way for the past thirty years. I have been wonderfully impressed with his humility, fearlessness, and sincerity. The small amount of money I have invested in him and his work, I suspect, has paid far bigger dividends than any other of the Lord's work in which I have had a part.

The greatest and most ripened field in the whole world, in my opinion, is among the Negroes in the United States. I have tried to make an estimate, which I think is conservative, of Brother Keeble's work, directly or indirectly in our country. I feel most sure that there have been some 25,000 people baptized in these twenty-five years by Brother Keeble and those preachers whom he has converted and developed. Just think, if you please, what we could do in the next generation if we can turn out men at our colored Bible school who could do, let's say, only one-half as much as Brother Keeble has been able to accomplish.

I have kept in close touch with this Bible School through Brother Elrod and Brother Holt and others. It is my opinion that it has about as good a

114

Athens Clay Pullias, Marshall Keeble, J. W. Brents, Percy Ricks

Preachers attending the N.C.I. annual lectureship

start as the old Nashville Bible School had fifty years ago. This makes it most interesting to calculate just what we can do among the colored people in the next fifty years.

There must be at least one thousand congregations throughout this country that would not have been in existence had it not been for the training boys and girls received from the old Bible School or David Lipscomb College. I think it conservative to say that there are at least one hundred thousand people in the Church of Christ today that would not have been had a congregation not been started in their community. I mention this to show the possibilities of the colored school. The colored people have quite an advantage because they will get the full support of the thousands of white congregations when colored preachers go into their midst.

I remember well one of the things that Brother David Lipscomb was interested in as much as any other in his last days was a school for the Negroes. It was he who encouraged me more than anyone to become interested in a school for the Negroes. It was he, also, who asked Brother Hammond and me to go to Silver Point, Tennessee, and investigate a colored school there. When we had made our report to him he put his approval on it and it was one of his last articles that appeared in the *Gospel Advocate* during his life time.

There is before us now the greatest opportunity we have ever had to extend the cause of Christ among the colored people of our United States. Let's use this opportunity.

In 1942, the fame of Marshall Keeble had grown wherever the church had been established. After Keeble became president of the Nashville Christian Institute, his reputation grew apace in the Negro community and among the Caucasian Christians. The praise of the school continually appearing in the *Gospel Advocate* obscured the harsh realities of the old Ashcraft building and the none too attractive physical surroundings.

During the early years of Keeble's ministry, his great popularity among white people aroused some suspicion among the Negroes. Until recent years the number of Negroes with even a junior college education was small indeed. But when he became the head of a school, his stature with his own race was enhanced. Keeble had been welcomed on the Lipscomb and Freed-Hardeman campuses for years. Being a school man put Keeble in wide demand everywhere with his new prestige as an educator.

A. M. Burton was planning ahead in 1944 for a larger school and better surroundings than the outmoded Ashcraft building. In 1944, he said that $60,000 had been set aside to that end. At the same time he was negotiating for a thousand acre tract of land in Sumner County to project agricultural training along with the Bible school, but nothing ever came of that plan because the white people in the community didn't want the school and worked against it. Brother Burton, instead, gave $50,000 toward a new building on the grounds of the Ashcraft school.

It would be a mistake to suppose Burton spent a major part of his time building a financial empire. It would be equally erroneous to think that his major contributions to Christian education came through his generous gifts to David Lipscomb College. In 1944, he wrote to the *Gospel Advocate*: "The good work that we have been able to accomplish at the Nashville Christian Institute for our colored people during the past ten years has been the most satisfying joy of my life."

Beginning in January 1944, the Negro brotherhood started an annual lectureship at the Nashville Christian Institute. The lectureship was suggested by Burton. An eight weeks Bible training course was conducted in the school. About forty preachers attended the lectures. The tuition fee was six dollars. The visiting preachers were housed and fed on the grounds.

The Negro preachers were trained by the best Christian educators that Nashville afforded at that time. Such men as S. H. Hall, B. C. Goodpasture, A. C. Pullias, J. P. Sanders, A. R. Holton, Willard Collins, and H. Leo Boles appeared on the program. Mrs. Lambert Campbell taught a class in the art of public speaking. They gave her $100 and she gave it back to the school. The whole venture was a grand success. A. R. Holton and H. Leo Boles suggested the lectureship become an annual affair running concurrently with the January lectureship of David Lipscomb College so visiting lecturers could appear on the Nashville Christian Institute program.

Never was so much realized from so little. The pittance of support that the Nashville Christian Institute received paid enormous dividends in the few years of its existence. Much of the support for the school was raised by Marshall Keeble. The school never had an endowment, and there were times when not a cent was left in the bank to pay teacher salaries. Then Keeble would take to the road to raise money. W. E. Brightwell put it like this—"Where will the next ton of coal come from? The food does not come by air lift, but it sometimes comes through gifts by friends, and of course, those gifts, often belated, cannot be calculated with accuracy too far in advance."

Though money was short, the school did not lack in teaching talent. The school faculty included such men as E. H. Ijams, Lacy H. Elrod, A. M. Burton, E. W. McMillan, and S. P. Pittman. In the first fifty years of this century, a large number of

Negro churches of Christ were established. In 1900 only one loyal church was meeting and that one was in the home of Alexander Campbell. The help Caucasians gave to establish congregations is a matter of record. From the beginning the support of the Nashville Christian Institute has been generously shared by white Christians.

The first graduation exercises of the Nashville Christian Institute were conducted June 10, 1945, in the Jefferson Street church of Christ and the Nashville Christian Institute school auditorium. The graduation sermon was preached by A. L. Cassius, minister of the Compton Avenue church of Christ in Los Angeles, California. The commencement address was delivered by G. E. Steward, minister of the Oklahoma City church of Christ. M. F. Holt led the invocation prayer and P. H. Black gave the benediction. General Andrew Jackson was the valedictorian and Vanderbilt Sardian Lewis, the salutatorian. The members of that graduation class also included Mary A. Russell, Robert Woods, Mary Carpenter, Anna Gilbert, and Charles Edward Woods.

Thousands of church members best remember Keeble accompanied by two or three preacher boys in the forties and fifties when he travelled across the country holding gospel meetings and raising money to operate his school. He conducted a meeting in Chattanooga, Tennessee, that closed July 14, 1946, after a four weeks stand. Crowds of from fifteen hundred to two thousand attended every night. The Chattanooga *Times* ran a special feature on the Keeble meeting. A part of what happened is best described by a *Times* reporter:

Two eleven-year-old colored "preachers" and an "old-timer" of fourteen are laying down the gospel law to overflow crowds at the church of Christ tent meeting here and making them like it.

They are proteges of Marshall Keeble, nationally famous Negro evangelist. Not even the Quiz Kids have better memories. Every night the crowd at Third Street and Orchard Knob is astounded to hear the trio, speaking five minutes each, supplement their scheduled talks by rattling off a chapter or two of Scripture.

"They've been traveling with me for a year now," Keeble says, "because they demonstrate unusual ability." All three are enrolled at the Nashville Christian Institute, of which Keeble is president.

William Robinson and Leroy Blackman are both eleven and from Decatur, Alabama. They were baptized together and started preaching the same day. Each has more than his share of stage presence and poise. William, a slightly-built youngster, has a voice like Orson Wells.

A third member of the trio is fourteen-year-old Hassen Reed, of Atonka, Oklahoma. Sunday afternoon he recited all of the second chapter of Acts to a steaming hot, but impressed, gathering.

"William, do you know all of the second chapter of Acts?" Brother Keeble asked last night.

"Yes, sir," William answered, dutifully.

"Do you know it, Leroy?" Brother Keeble turned to his young evangelist.

Leroy thought that one over for a while, then said, defensively, "No, but I know all the fifth chapter of Matthew."

C. W. Scott, local evangelist, has been prominent in conducting the meetings here. They are sponsored by the church of Christ in the city.

In June 1945, the white church brought Marshall Keeble to Natchez, Mississippi, for a meeting, accompanied by four of his "preaching boys." This was a previously untouched Negro mission field. Paul Tucker who was preaching for the white church in Natchez tells the story. James D. Willeford who was preaching in Carlsbad, New Mexico, was interested in preaching the gospel to the Negroes. He encouraged the Carlsbad church to send Keeble to Natchez for a meeting. The white people in Natchez put up the tent and the wind blew it down. Keeble told them—"Now let me put it up. You brethren don't know how to put it up anyhow."

The relationship of the Southern Caucasian and Negro often presents a puzzle. In the "Old South" Natchez, Mississippi, was divided into sections. There was the plantation mansion. The homes of the Negroes were built on the grounds to the side and rear of the mansion. Such an arrangement presented no social dilemma. The sight is still a common one in Natchez. Keeble never faced a problem with the white people once he learned their social customs.

Paul Tucker carried a picture of Keeble to run it as a part of advertising of the meeting. But the Natchez newspaper would not carry the picture of a Negro at that time. The boys accompanying Keeble were Robert McBride, Hassen Reed, Robert Wood, and Fred Gray. Keeble and the boys walked all over Natchez distributing hand bills in the Negro homes. A new Negro church grew out of this effort, but this was an "oft told" tale in Keeble's preaching career.

Marshall Keeble was in a meeting in Pecos, Texas, in the fall of 1951. During that meeting Billie Sol Estes was restored to the church. That dated the beginning of a friendship between Marshall Keeble and Billie Sol Estes that continues for many years. A part of the story deserves telling. The tuition of Negro boys going to the Nashville Christian Institute was paid by the Texan. When a gas bill or some indebtedness would run up around $500, Keeble would tell Mary Campbell, "Phone Sol and tell him we need $500." Shortly the money would arrive. Other than this kind of help Estes never gave money to the school. The Nashville

119

Christian Institute did invest on his advice some capital in real property secured by first mortgages that is a sound investment. Billie Sol Estes had no other financial connections with the Nashville Christian Institute.

In the early sixties, cataracts were slowly blinding Keeble. He had to undergo surgery. One of the finest surgeons in the South, Dr. John Ralph Rice, removed the cataract from his left eye in General Hospital. The attendant nurses were under orders to keep him under strict surveillance to prevent his tearing the bandages from his eye. In an unguarded moment unfortunately, he tore away the bandage and destroyed the vision in his left eye. Dr. Rice agreed to perform similar surgery in Vanderbilt University on the other eye provided someone watch Keeble every moment around the clock.

That chore was discharged with "love and devotion" by Lambert and Mary Campbell, and Laura Keeble. They sat by his bedside in three hour watches. The first person Dr. Rice arranged for Keeble to see through a narrow slit in the bandage was his friend, Mary Campbell. Dr. Rice performed the surgery without cost to Keeble. Billie Sol Estes instructed Mary Campbell to buy Keeble the best glass eye in Nashville. They looked at every "glass eye" stocked in Nashville. With his never failing humor, Keeble finally found one—"I can see through this one—I'll take it." In addition to the "glass eye," Estes told Mary Campbell to buy Keeble several pairs of glasses so he would never have to be without them. "I don't court you to make a friend out of you," Keeble once said. This is the story of Keeble's life. He makes friends and never loses them, and he counts Billie Sol Estes as a friend.

Ira North is one of Keeble's friends. In the spring of 1952, when North was in Baton Rouge, Louisiana, working on a doctorate program in the University of Louisiana, Keeble came to Baton Rouge to hold a meeting supported by the Chapel Avenue church in Nashville, and the Convention Street church in Baton Rouge. Brother North described some of the details of the meeting—

The white brethren here have done a great job advertising the meeting. Spot announcements were purchased on the radio, large ads were run for weeks in the leading Negro paper, stories of Brother Keeble and his "boy preachers" were run in the three leading newspapers. Some fifty white disciples visited colored homes and distributed thousands of hand bills. Fifty-six ladies volunteered to call on the colored residences and give them a personal invitation to the meeting. Window cards were placed in the colored businesses of the city, and Brother Keeble and his boys appeared over our local radio program.

Left to right, standing: Hassen Reed, Robert McBride. Left to right, seated:
Robert Wood, Marshall Keeble, Fred Gray.

121

A. M. Burton kept a personal file of information on Marshall Keeble that he treasured. One item is a letter from Ira North about the meeting:

Dear Brother Burton:

Knowing of your great interest in the Nashville Christian Institute I thought you would enjoy reading the enclosed article.

We had a great meeting with Brother Keeble—have already secured a regular colored preacher and are planning some way to provide a modest building soon. We now have sixteen colored members. Brother Keeble is so pleased with the outlook for the school.

Respectfully,
IRA NORTH

There is no end to the surprises in Keeble's long preaching career. He breaks all attendance records with his lectures in college auditoriums. Large municipal auditoriums overflow their capacity when Keeble comes to town. Church auditoriums even in his old age, are jammed from wall to wall and flow over into adjoining class rooms and all other spaces in the building; some are even turned away. In 1954, Keeble conducted a meeting in Beamsville, Ontario, Canada, with two of the "preacher boys." No Negroes lived in the areas. When the invitation came, Keeble asked Mary Campbell, "Do they know I am 'Negro?'"

She told him, "Of course, they know it!" But Keeble wouldn't be content until a long distance telephone call assured Keeble they knew him. "Who is it that doesn't know Keeble among the churches of Christ?" This experience became one of Keeble's living memories and he wrote about it—"There was no unpleasant mess or bad feeling. Thank God." The Beamsville High School added another thrill to Keeble's life—he was invited to deliver the baccalaureate sermon to the graduating class. Such incidents are legion. Keeble is incredible. Any person who tries to tell the Keeble story is frustrated by the inadequacy of words to do justice to the magnitude of his performances.

Among those who served the Nashville Christian Institute with devotion and sacrifice, is E. Frank N. Tharpe, who was principal in 1945. Tharpe was born in Memphis, Tennessee, and received his secondary education in the public schools of that city where he was graduated from LeMoyne High School. Tharpe attended Howe Institute and Walden College and earned the B. A. and M. S. degrees in A. & I. College in Nashville.

O. H. Boatright, who had been a teacher in the school, became its principal in 1949. Boatright graduated from Fisk University

122

with an A. B. degree in English and Business Law. He was born in Haywood County, Tennessee. Boatright started preaching for the Jackson Street church who provided a part of his support.

The Nashville Christian Institute has been guided by three presidents—Marshall Keeble, Lucien Palmer, and Willie T. Cato. The school had two other principals after Tharpe and Boatright—James Dennis, a Negro, and C. B. Laws, a white man.

Among the teachers who came to the Nashville Christian Institute and gave a full measure of love and devotion, J. W. Brents is deserving of great credit. The young Negroes who came under his training were called by him "my boys." The students loved J. W. Brents. He received his support mainly from white churches in widely separated places. Brents had been a great evangelist in his day and served out his last year in one of the greatest roles in his life teaching in the Nashville Christian Institute.

Brents wrote in 1956, after nine years of service as head of the Bible Department of the Nashville Christian Institute:

From its beginning the school has had a hard struggle to survive. But year after year as the brotherhood has become acquainted with the work it is doing they have made the burden lighter. . . . Each student is given Bible work each day. Young men come to the school from all parts of our country to study the Bible under Christian teachers. When I began work with the school it was my ambition to live long enough that I might assist in training at least 500 preachers. I am sure this goal has been reached.

J. W. Brents was teaching his eighteenth year in the school when he died on October 20, 1963.

The name of Mary Campbell (Mrs. Lambert Campbell) ranks second to none in the eventful life of Marshall Keeble. Her service to the school is best remembered by the programs that students of the Nashville Christian Institute offered to the general public. The programs were first presented in the Central church of Christ and next in the War Memorial Auditorium—always to packed houses. The programs were later presented in Alumni Auditorium of David Lipscomb College on the first Sunday afternoon in May by invitation of President Athens Clay Pullias saving the Nashville Christian Institute the $100 rental fee charged for the War Memorial Auditorium. Large sums of money for the Nashville Christian Institute were raised on these occasions. The last programs of this kind were presented in the Marshall Keeble Hall on the Institute campus. Keeble taught the "preacher boys" what to say; Mary Campbell them *how* to say their lessons. They were called "Sister Campbell's boys."

In the first sixteen years of Nashville Christian Institute operation, thirty-five hundred students passed through the high school and elementary departments. Although the plans to expand the school were altered by circumstances, in 1955, the Ashcraft school building was remodelled. In the spring of this same year, construction began on a two-story combination auditorium and dormitory to accommodate one hundred and forty students with living quarters for a supervisor. A combination gymnasium and auditorium floor was designed to seat a thousand people. Niles E. Yearwood, contractor, estimated the cost of building and furnishing the new construction would run to $200,000. For the first time, the school had facilities that were partially adequate.

In 1955, two hundred and thirty-four boys and girls had received diplomas from the school. Of that number, ninety-seven were preachers who, in that period of time, had baptized 2,750 of their own race. Some 2,500 adults attended the annual lectureship from its beginning.

The story of the Nashville Christian Institute cannot be fully told without including Lucien Palmer and Willie T. Cato. Lucien Palmer, a graduate of David Lipscomb College worked in the Nigerian mission field between 1954 and 1958. He finally returned to the states because of the illness of his son.

Lucien Palmer was invited to the office of A. M. Burton, Chairman of the Nashville Christian Institute Board of Directors. Keeble was growing older, and a new president was being sought for the Nashville Christian Institute. Athens Clay Pullias, Secretary-Treasurer of the Board, also scheduled conferences with Palmer concerning his becoming president of Nashville Christian Institute. He accepted the challenge to become president of the school effective July, 1958. Marshall Keeble was retained as President Emeritus of the school.

Lucien Palmer's tenure was short lived. Otis Gatewood invited Palmer to come to Michigan to help launch Michigan Christian College. Keeble and Palmer made a great team. The school prospered under their leadership. A mutual respect for each other deepened into a close friendship. The Board of Directors were reluctant to release Palmer.

Palmer was convinced a personal friend of his would do an equally good job. He gave his full recommendation to Willie T. Cato for the position. Cato was well known to President Pullias.

Ezell, Keeble, Palmer

C. A. O. Essien

Keeble seated between Upkom village
tribal chiefs

Keeble appointed Nigerian tribal chief

After careful consideration, Cato accepted the challenge to replace Palmer. Again Marshall Keeble fully measured up and gave Willie Cato the fullest encouragement and support.

Beginning in January, 1959, Willie Cato has served as president. Keeble and Cato have worked closely together for the past eight years for the cause of Christian education. Palmer wrote about his successor—"I will always be glad that it was my privilege to recommend him and to urge him to become president." Cato justly deserves, and will rightfully receive, a great measure of honor for his unselfish devotion to the cause of Christian Education among the Negro youth. No other white person has worked as long in daily personal contact with Marshall Keeble as Willie Cato. What a great team they have made! The Nashville Christian Institute closed its doors in the spring of 1967. Keeble honors his younger associate and often speaks words in his praise.

Other than A. M. Burton, no other person outside the Nashville Christian Institute staff has worked closer and longer with the school than Athens Clay Pullias. Pullias, longtime Nashville Christian Institute board member, took over in 1951 as Secretary-Treasurer of the school from J. E. Acuff, long time friend and benefactor of Christian Negroes. Brother Acuff's work goes back to a teaching program he conducted in the Jackson Street church in the early years of this century. Marshall Keeble regards President Pullias as one of the greatest friends of his life, and acknowledges his invaluable help and advice in conducting the affairs of the Nashville Christian Institute. Often he tells his Negro associates: "You don't realize the value of the man."

Marshall Keeble publicly announced, March 16, 1967, in the *Gospel Advocate,* that the Nashville Christian Institute would close its doors on June 2, 1967. The changing times faced the school with what now appears to be insurmountable obstacles. It's the same old story. To meet the continual accreditation standards set forth by the Tennessee State Board of Education, millions of dollars, and acres of land are only some of the problems that plagued the Board of Directors.

The school has suffered a slowly declining enrollment. The teacher-salaries were less than half that of the city schools. The magnificent public school complexes with highly trained personnel naturally drew the talented students. The decision to close the school was reached by the Board of Directors after a special committee was appointed to make a careful survey and to submit their recommendations.

The Nashville Christian Institute was a going concern as long as A. M. Burton and Marshall Keeble were around to keep it on its feet. The plain truth is that A. M. Burton became primarily interested in the Nashville Christian Institute as a training ground for Negro preachers under the talented guidance of Marshall Keeble. Christians of both races feel sad about ending the school. Keeble has one answer for all—"If you had supported us with your money and given us your children, we would be so big now you couldn't close us down."

A few weeks before his passing, A. M. Burton and Marshall Keeble created the Burton-Keeble Fund to educate Negro boys and girls in David Lipscomb College. It is a long way back down the vista of time when A. M. Burton walked the streets of North Nashville selling insurance. The desire of A. M. Burton to elevate and dignify the Negro through Christian education was deep and sincere. Only eternity can calculate the influence for good that A. M. Burton and Marshall Keeble accomplished in their span of years on earth.

127

CHAPTER X

Around the World

While Keeble was holding a meeting in Atlanta, Georgia, on his seventieth birthday, he wrote a note to the *Advocate*: "I mean to wear out on the battlefield." Keeble is now in his ninetieth year; and after wearing out several battlefields is still going strong. When most men still living at his age are retired to their comfortable armchairs, at eighty-four Keeble was circling the earth in a jet airliner. It would be difficult to discover a fitting climax to end the Keeble story. There is little question that his visits to the Holy Land, to Nigeria, and finally around the world brought a great measure of joy to the mighty, little gospel warrior.

The occasion for Keeble's first trip abroad was to visit the church in Nigeria. Lucien Palmer and his family were engaged from 1954 through 1959 in the Nigerian work. After Palmer became Dean of Michigan Christian College, he planned to re-visit in 1960 the Nigerian work as a part of a large plan to help keep mission work alive around the world. He thought of having Keeble to accompany him though Keeble was eighty-two and slowly going blind because of cataracts. Palmer publicly suggested the trip in April of 1959 during the Nashville Christian Institute Lectureship. Some of Keeble's friends wondered if he would be able to stand the rigors of the trip. Brother Burton was dead set against Keeble's going, and felt Keeble should not go because of his advanced age. He told Keeble: "They are going to kill you. You are worth too much to the church to be running around all over the world taking all kinds of chances." Keeble said his old friend had tears in his eyes and reaching all the while in his back pocket for a thousand dollars to give on the trip. Mary and Lambert Campbell supported the idea from the first and became the treasurer for the Keeble-Palmer travel fund.

There is a story behind Keeble and Palmer's trip to Africa that deserves recording which goes back to the dark days during World War II when American boys were fighting and dying all around the world. The elders of the Lawrence Avenue church of Christ were saddened to see them caught up in the whirlwind of war and scattered to the distant battle fronts far removed from the church

Keeble and Palmer at tomb of Jesus

Keeble and Palmer in front of Dome of the Rock

and constantly exposed to the attendent evils of camp life. As so many churches did, they began writing personal letters to their boys.

When the men of the Lawrence Avenue church met for the regular monthly business meeting on the night of May 2, 1944, they were not aware of its historic significance, and that thousands of people would be brought to Christ as a result was a thought far removed from their minds that night. They decided to prepare a Bible course for young men in the armed services. With the assistance of talented members, Gordon Turner, minister of the church, immediately began the preparation of the Bible Correspondence Course consisting of twenty-six lessons that scanned the entire Bible. The information about the correspondence course went out to all parts of the world where service men were stationed. One of the correspondence courses fell into the hands of Miss Anna-Maria Braun of Germany. She had established the Internationales Korrespondenz-Buro in 1945 to promote the learning of languages through letter exchange between pen pals living in different parts of the world. She expressed her interest in the Bible Correspondence Course in a letter to the Lawrence Avenue church.

In July of 1948 a letter came from a native Nigerian, C. A. O. Essien, requesting an enrollment in the course. His return address was unusual—Ibiaku, Ikot Usen, Ibione, Itu, Nigeria, West Africa. It has never been established how Essien came to be on Miss Braun's list of correspondents. Anyhow, she referred him to the Lawrence Avenue church for the Bible Correspondence Course. In later exchange of letters, Essien wrote that he had taken other Bible correspondence courses from the States, but none had so enlightened him in the study of the Bible.

Soon after receiving the lessons, Essien began preaching the gospel among the natives in his village. Soon a vast restoration movement was underway. Essien started a stream of letters to the Lawrence Avenue church pleading for white missionaries. He wrote: "We can teach our people, but we need teaching ourselves. Send men to teach us and we shall take Nigeria for the truth."

The Lawrence Avenue elders sent Boyd Reese and Eldred Nichols to Nigeria "to spy out the land," and their report was glowing with favor. It was now clear that the Lawrence Avenue church had to take charge of the work, and a call went forth for qualified preachers. At first no one was willing to make the sacri-

Keeble Hall—Nigerian Christian Secondary School

Nigerian hospital

Nigerian interpreter and Keeble

131

fice. Then Howard Horton and his wife, Mildred, stepped forth; and they were joined by Jimmy Johnson and his wife, Rosa Lee. Both families arrived in Nigeria in the closing days of November of 1952. There were others to follow—Eugene Peden and his family. Then in October of 1954, Lucien Palmer and his family moved to Nigeria. What a success story it turned out to be!

Lucien Palmer summed up the efforts of the Nigerian work and the phenomenal progress that had been made since the beginning of 1952. There were in 1964 five hundred churches of Christ, two Bible training schools, ten elementary schools with an enrollment of three thousand pupils and one hundred teachers. This is only a meager part of the story that forms the backdrop for Keeble's visit for Nigeria.

While Keeble was in a meeting in 1930 at Plant City, Florida, he was visited by J. M. McCaleb, who expressed at that time a hope that Negro evangelists would be trained to work among their own race in Africa. Keeble little knew then that one day he would be winging his way across the Atlantic at almost the speed of sound to visit the land of his nativity and to preach the gospel to the Africans.

In preparation for the trip, a Mission Lectureship Workshop was conducted at North Central Christian College in Rochester, Michigan, as a training program for mature preachers. As the lectureship closed, Marshall Keeble and Lucien Palmer boarded a jet, June 11, 1962, in New York, whose destination was London, England. Their planned itinerary carried them to Paris, France, Rome, Italy, Cairo, Egypt, Beirut, Lebanon, Damascus, Syria, and through Palestine from Dan to Beersheba. Palmer and Keeble were in Palestine from June 22 through June 28. Keeble suffered his only illness in Jerusalem, and Palmer feared for a while it would be a fatal illness. Keeble snapped back and went the rest of the trip without missing half a step.

After their Palestinian tour, they returned to Rome by way of Athens, Greece, and flew to Cane, Nigeria. They travelled by automobile to Port Harcourt where they were met by the missionaries and travelled eighty miles into the bush country to the Bible College at Ukpom. The following address of welcome was made the Asutan Ekpe church of Christ to Palmer and Keeble on their first visit to the Asutan Ekpe District:

We, the entire congregational members of Asutan Ekpe Church of Christ greet, and welcome you to our midst with delight.

132

It is, indeed, a happy event that it falls a very good turn for the American Brothers to send you out over to this country to see and arrange things of vital importance against future developments, and progress.

On this special mission, we suggest it might not take you a long stay in Nigeria as we can imagine.

We hope it would not be out of place if in this short address we enumerate for kind consideration and action of our new American Brothers some of our dire needs which have placed this very Community backward which failure to consider, has left this Community in a bad position.

In the first instant, we are grateful to all American Brothers who work among us in leading us aright with the Gospel messages which is the first step of Christian life.

Still yet, there are other amenities which we are sure if attended to will add more progress to the entire Community.

To point out a few, we have been striving (1) for an establishment of a Technical Secondary School in this very Community through the help of our American Brothers. (2) Also Maternity Clinic and (3) Some other Grammar Schools in the area.

The attached copies are the appeal presented to our Home American Brethren in respect of this special request in which we hope you would add more efforts to see that the need is supplied.

We are particularly optimistic that with our able Missionaries the tide will reverse in our favour. That very soon our reply to this special request of Technical School will be considered.

Once again, we greet and welcome you to this Community, and wish you God's guidance in the demand.

We are:—

B. E. IMAH

For and on behalf of Asutan Ekpe District Congregations.

Keeble preached day and night during his entire stay. Nothing in Keeble's long life thrilled him like those African days and nights. On the eve of Keeble's departure for the United States, he preached at Iket Usen where Essien first started the work. A welcome was held for Keeble in the Iket school building attended by several hundred people including the district officials. The afternoon was turned into a preaching service and fifty-five persons were baptized. At the conclusion of this service, Keeble was made an honorary chief of their tribe by the people and the visiting dignitaries. Whatever Keeble tells about in his long life, this is, by far one of the greatest thrills of his life. The story of Marshall Keeble's visit to the Holy Land and Nigeria is told in Mary Campbell's book—*From Mule Back to Super Jet.*

Lucien Palmer was elated with the success of the trip. Keeble's presence among the Africans was a deeply moving experience for them and especially when they became aware of his advanced age. Palmer said even when they were returning home, he began entertaining a secret hope that Keeble and he should have a second opportunity to return to Africa. Keeble told the story that when they were airborne for New York on a Sunday, Lucien had

133

planned for the occasion. They took the Lord's supper together at better than 30,000 feet. The stewardess saw them partaking of the emblems and was curious to inquire what they were up to.

The Christians in the Detroit area arranged a big home-coming for Marshall Keeble and Lucien Palmer. The Ford Auditorium was booked and a packed house awaited the arrival of Marshall Keeble who was in for another surprise of his life. They took their seats on the elevator stage stationed on a lower level from the main floor of the auditorium. Lucien Palmer, Willie T. Cato, and Otis Gatewood were sitting on the stage with Marshall Keeble. The stage slowly rose from the pit in view of the audience. Keeble was given a standing ovation by the assembled crowd. Cato said in all of his life he had never seen members of the church do that before.

Two years passed before Marshall Keeble and Lucien Palmer accompanied by Houston T. Ezell made their trip around the world. Plans were carefully laid. Money had been left over from the first trip, and the problem of financing the second journey presented no problem. A. M. Burton had not favored the first trip because he feared for Keeble's life. But he was adamant when the second one was brought up and would not be reconciled to the idea. But Keeble is a stubborn man when his mind is made up and he meant to make that second trip. Keeble was just recovering from a spell of sickness which gave cause for some concern.

Palmer and Keeble were scheduled to leave for Nigeria following the Michigan Christian College lectureship. Houston T. Ezell and his wife were visiting with the Palmers and attending the lectureship. Palmer began talking with Ezell about making the journey with them. After a great deal of on-the-spot discussion, Ezell agreed he should go provided they would stop off by Korea to see the work there. The Korean work was a special project of the Vultee church where Ezell serves as an elder. He wanted Palmer to make comparisons, and he was going to do the same between the Nigerian and Korean efforts. They agreed after the journey the two fields were just about a draw.

The day of departure was just one week away. Edwin H. Enzor, elder of the Arlington, Virginia church of Christ, assured them he would make all the necessary arrangements. Houston Ezell drove to Nashville to take his vaccinations and set some of his business affairs in order. He was back in New York on time to take off with his friends. Their departure was on October 23,

134

Nigerian bush country church

Graduating class of Upkom village Bible College

1962. Their arrival was planned to coincide with the Nigerian Lectureship scheduled to begin on October 29.

Lucien Palmer, who had served as the President of the Nigerian Christian School, was returning to help make plans to open the new Nigerian Christian Secondary School. Keeble gave all of his time in training classes with the Nigerian preachers and conducting gospel meetings. He spoke daily to hundreds in the market places, down by the river side, in mud houses, and under brush arbors. Lucien Palmer and Houston Ezell were out beating the bushes looking for a location for the new secondary school. They were three weeks in Nigeria. Ezell said he would never forget a statement Keeble made when they were visiting the elaborate compounds of the Catholic Church and other religious groups with their fine schools and hospitals to gain some idea about what they could best do.

Keeble remarked on that occasion: "I tell you fellows—that's what is wrong with the church of Christ. These churches get here fifty years ahead of us—get these children and train them, and line up the people and indoctrinate them. Then we send two missionaries over here and try to head them off."

Two Bible colleges are now operating in eastern Nigeria—one in Ukpom and the other in Onicha Ngwa. The Bible colleges are more nearly the equivalent of a Sunday school especially designed to train preachers. Houston Ezell returned to Ukpom in the fall of 1966 in the Abok District to supervise the completion of the buildings for the Nigerian Christian Secondary School which is equal to an American high school and the first year of college. Some twenty buildings are located on the campus just across the road from the Ukpom Bible College. The main administrative building on the secondary school campus is named Keeble Hall.

On this second trip the natives were begging Keeble for a hospital, and he told them that he would see about it. Ezell said that meant you would build them one. Palmer and Ezell tried to get Keeble to go easy on that point, but it didn't do much good. And when Keeble got back to the states, he started riding his brethren about that hospital. The first stages of that hospital are now in operation in Nigeria, and it is the only hospital in the world operated by members of the churches of Christ.

The hospital complex comprises a maternity clinic, operating amphitheater, two ward buildings for men and women, kitchen and

Marshall Keeble and Tan Keng Koon
in Singapore

A Korean Christian and
Marshall Keeble

Ezell, Keeble, Palmer in Korea

Keeble interpreter in Korea

laundry, and a morgue. Dr. Henry Farrar, M.D., has been working as a doctor and preacher in Nigeria since 1964. Dr. Farrar returned to the States in July of 1967 along with other white missionaries to await the resolving of the civil war that is now troubling the Nigerians.

The Nigerians loved Keeble because he was black and an American and cared enough about them to come back to see them. When Keeble first went to Nigeria the people began crying when they met him. Keeble asked Palmer: "What are they crying about Brother Palmer? Looks like they are sorry they met me." He learned their tears came out of respect for his old age.

Houston Ezell summed up some facts about Keeble that have been of long standing: "Keeble integrated Christians and we integrated with Keeble long before they started talking about integration. Keeble broke down barriers by being willing to be a brother and not trying to be a spectacle of some kind."

The trip was not made without incident. Houston Ezell was thrown from a motor scooter and suffered fractured ribs causing him no little pain. After leaving Nigeria, their next major step was in Addis Ababa, Ethiopia. There were anxious hours on that trip. One of the props went out on the big four-motored plane, and a second motor was not working properly. An Englishman sitting beside Ezell was frantic. The Englishman told him that they were approaching one of the most treacherous landing fields in the world situated right between two mountains. The Ethiopian capitol is located at a very high altitude. The propellers were icing up. Then when the ice would loosen from the props, the ice would be thrown against the cabin. Ezell said the way that Englishman kept running up and down the aisle to and from the pilot: "He liked to got me scared to death." But he said Keeble was sitting there "cool, calm, and collected."

They learned another great lesson in Ethiopia. When the church expressed a wish to send missionaries into Ethiopia, this is what they were told: "We don't mind you preaching the gospel to our people, but what else are you going to do for them?" As a result the church started a school for the "deaf and speechless." The daughter of King Haile Selassie had a child who was thus afflicted. She gave the ground for the new school, and loaned the church $24,000 American dollars to start the building program.

Their itinerary carried them from Africa to Pakistan and then

138

into Bombay, India. Lucien Palmer was violently ill and running a dangerously high fever, and they were afraid of being quarantined. When his condition worsened, they sent for an Indian doctor who spoke beautiful English; and to their great relief was a fine physician. He diagnosed the case as "strep throat" and Palmer was on his way to recovery.

Keeble was a veteran traveller by now. He never got sick and accuses Palmer of taking all his medicine that he was supposed to take if he got sick. Keeble remarked that in America there were "red caps" who carried your luggage. But he said on that trip he had two "white caps" to carry his luggage. Ezell said he never saw Keeble upset but once, and that was in Bombay, India. The custom officials caught some native smugglers just ahead of them. Keeble and his party had their luggage searched. They started cramming Keeble's clothes back in the suitcase to hasten him on down the line. Keeble was stubborn. He wouldn't budge until he had packed every article neatly folded into the place where it belonged grumbling every second at the custom people. From Bombay, they travelled to Thailand, Singapore, Hong Kong, and finally to Korea. The Koreans were fascinated with Keeble, and he preached his heart out to them and baptized a large number. They returned home by way of the Hawaiian Islands. Keeble told them in Los Angeles that he went out the front door and came in the back door. The people in Los Angeles wanted to know what Keeble meant by that "back door" business?

All of this is now history in Keeble's life. When Keeble reflects back over his long and fruitful life, both tears and happy laughter reflect his emotions. Keeble is a great believer in Christian colleges, and he is thrilled that the doors of all the Christian colleges are open to everyone. He tells white audiences: "I see your daughter with a little African baby in her arms. I shed tears looking at the little girl just out of college helping a mother wash and clean her baby." Keeble would add: "Your daughter has gone beyond you because you didn't go to college." Keeble said many a man would go down in his pocket for a hundred or a thousand dollars when he told that story The Keeble story is still going on as the little gospel preacher goes all over the nation preaching to great audiences and baptizing people in large numbers.

And he said: "That's why I am living today. My work has been such a pleasure." During a recent meeting in the Jackson

Street church, a little Negro boy finished his sermonette, and in complimenting Brother Keeble, said: "Brother Keeble is living on borrowed time and I hope it's not mine!" Keeble said it is like this: "when my time is up, the Lord will let me know. I've been ready. When I have to go, I'll go. But they are going to know I've been here." In their last days, both N. B. Hardeman and A. M. Burton sent for Keeble to come to them. He comforted Brother Hardeman who was sad because he could preach no longer. Keeble remarked: "You've already said enough if you never say another word."

Marshall Keeble and his wife, Laura, are living in a modest beautiful new home in the rolling hills just north of the city of Nashville. A new interstate highway forced them from their home where they had lived for many years on Scovell Street near Fisk University. His health is good with the exception of a diabetic condition and his mind is clear. Mary and Lambert Campbell along with Laura look after his state of health. Maybe Brother Keeble won't pass away for a while, but just turn into a rare piece of ebony and stay around a little longer. So good-bye for now old friend. We don't expect to see the likes of you around here again.

INDEX

Parables, 97
Pepperdine College, xiii
Pittman, S. P., 9
Pullias, A. C., 93, 123, 126
Pullias, Charley M., 11, 50

Ramsey, John T., 84
Reed, Hassen, 119
Restoration Movement, ix, 1, 3, 5, 80
Rice, Dr. John Ralph, 120
Richardson, "Pop," 62
Ricks, Percy, 70
Ridgely, Tennessee, 78

St. Petersburg, Florida, 62
Sanders, J. P., 93
Selassie, King Haile, 138
Seventh Day Adventist, 75
Sewell, E. G., 9
Shaw, T. J., 4
Showalter, G. P. H., 74
Silver Point Church, 32
Silver Point School, 24, 26, 27, 28
Smith, Lonnie, 62, 91, 108
Soap factory, 17
Southern Practical Institute, 30
Southwestern Christian College, 23, 31
Speer, Dr. Glover, 60
Steward, G. E., 91, 118
Stone, Barton W., ix, 2, 3
Sturgis, Mississippi, 51
Sunday, Billy, 41

Swanson, Bishop, 66
Sweeney, Lee, 49

Tampa, Florida, 56
Taylor, Preston, 6, 16, 17
Tennessee State Prison, xii, 98
Tharpe, E. Frank N., 122
Tiner, Hugh H., xii, xiii, 74
Tucker, Paul, 108, 119
Tuggle, Annie C., 7, 26, 27, 28, 30

"Uncle Tom," 41

Valdosta, Georgia, 62, 64
Vaughan, J. Roy, 59
Vaughner, John, 68, 88, 89, 94

Walden University, 3
Wall, Willie D., 30
Wallace, Foy E., Jr., 64
Washington, Booker T., 21, 41, 85
Willeford, James D., 119
Williams, Alonzo, 90
Winston, J. S., 82
WLAC, xiii, 56
Womack, Minnie, 18
Womack, Philistia, 19
Womack, S. W., xv, 1, 2, 4, 7, 8, 24, 83
Womack, Sally, 22
Wood, Robert, 119
World Fair Singer Bowl, xiv

Yearwood, Niles E., 124
Young, M. Norvel, 54